CONSTRUCTING ARCHITECTURE

Inès Lamunière is an exceptional architect, a committed educator and a generous colleague. In 1994, she and I were both invited to the Graduate School of Design at Harvard University as visiting professors, and we met in the design studios, where the areas assigned to our students were adjacent.

Our chance encounter evolved into a wonderful friendship based on our shared passion for teaching and practice. My partner Howard Sutcliffe and I have had the good fortune to visit many of Devanthéry et Lamunière Architects' accomplished built works, including schools, hospitals, office buildings, train stations, libraries, an opera house and private residences.

The EPFL Lausanne has been a home for Inès since her formative years as an architecture student up until her time as head of the architecture school. The institution has always invited the best visiting critics, scholars and practising architects from around the world to teach at its school alongside its distinguished faculty members, thus ensuring a vital and dynamic student experience. In 1977, Kenneth Frampton was one of many visiting professors and, in his studio, he encountered Inès Lamunière as a young architecture student. Frampton recalls Inès as a formidable presence, forever challenging his ideas about modernism. In 1994, she returned to the EPFL as a full professor, launching her stellar teaching career. The school enabled her to explore a broad range of

6 pressing issues, such as the role of integrative infrastructure and its relationship to city-building, rethinking the role of nature in urban environments, and embracing our contemporary perception of risk and danger and its impact on architecture. As chair of the EPFL's Department of Architecture from 2008 to 2011, Inès continued its legacy of inviting eminent visitors from around to world to engage directly with the students. Since 2014, Inès has shaped the future of the discipline through her remarkable PhD students. She has always been a demanding and rigorous academic and educator, posing tough, complex questions to her students and drawing on interdisciplinary design thinking to re-imagine a new future.

Inès has always been an activist within the architecture discipline, instigating and embracing positive change. As co-editor of the Geneva-based architecture journal *Faces – Journal d'architecture* for fifteen years, she played a vital role in disseminating ideas and projects. She served as a board member and champion of the Italian movement Archizoom and of the EPFL's Wish Foundation, advocating for women in the sciences and the humanities. In 2010, the EPFL launched an ambitious two-stage international competition for its new Learning Center, and Inès played a critical role in curating a list of international competition candidates. She also worked closely with the EPFL faculty administration and invited

external judges to help achieve a unanimous jury decision that led to the
construction of a new Rolex building by SANAA, which has revitalised
and transformed the EPFL campus.

In 2011, Inès Lamunière and Patrick Devanthéry received the prestigious Meret Oppenheim Prize from the Swiss Federal Art Commission for their rich and diverse body of award-winning work. The citation described their high degree of sensitivity in addressing challenging conditions, simultaneously connecting urban context and modernity. Inès Lamunière was also praised for inspiring several generations of young architects through her built work, her teaching and her ongoing contribution to the broader architectural discussion. In 2017, the Ministry of Culture of the French Republic made Inès Lamunière a Chevalier de l'Ordre des Arts et des Lettres, an honour for individuals who have distinguished themselves in their artistic field and the contribution they have made in France and in the world.

In 2016, I had the great pleasure of introducing Inès to a Canadian audience of practising architects and students of architecture, landscape and urban design at the University of Toronto. The title of her lecture was Constructing Architecture. She chose both words – "constructing" and "architecture" and fused them together to create a new set of relationships. The first word – constructing – is both a verb and noun. The verb

8 con.struct.ing means to build or erect something, typically a building. The noun con.struct.ing is linked to an idea or theory containing various conceptual elements. Constructing is inextricably linked to Inès Lamunière's distinguished career in which she always connects the construction of physical buildings with the building of ideas linked to research and to teaching the next generation of architects in Switzerland, Europe and North America. She focuses on the art of architecture and the practice of designing and constructing architecture through ideas, words, models and drawings, and ultimately through their physical form as buildings.

During her lecture, Inès shared recent work from dl-a designlab – architecture presenting an agriculture research station design with an exuberant use of colour and materiality, fusing and intertwining building and landscape. She also presented a flagship intergenerational housing project which, through the skilful use of innovative public space, connects families and seniors in one joyous complex comprising a day-care centre, medical facilities and restaurants.

Switzerland is a unique country with a small physical footprint and a large presence, with a very crowded landscape and many talented architects. Inès Lamunière is a uniquely gifted architect with a stellar body of work to her name, work that is probing and questioning, and has resulted in projects that tell us about our cities and our landscapes.

Lamunière has always been a strong academic leader and educator who has led by example, sharing her profound knowledge of the history and theory of architecture and giving her students a strong foundation. For nearly four decades, Inès has held an unwavering belief in the power of architecture to implement social and civic change and to maximise our environmental potential. Inès Lamunière is always Constructing Architecture and she is always reminding us that architecture impacts our society and touches lives in meaningful and profound ways.

Brigitte Shim
Principal Shim-Sutcliffe Architect
Professor, Faculty of Architecture, Landscape and Design, University of Toronto
Toronto,12 June, 2018

Le texte ne « commente » pas les images. Les images n'« illustrent » pas le texte : chacune a été seulement pour moi le départ d'une sorte de vacillement visuel, analogue peut-être à cette *perte de sens* que le Zen appelle un *satori* ; texte et images, dans leur entrelacs, veulent assurer la circulation, l'échange de ces signifiants : le corps, le visage, l'écriture et y lire le recul des signes.

Roland Barthes
L'Empire des signes, 1970

WORLDS

Laurent Stadler: Some practice first as architects before becoming teachers. You did the opposite. How did that come about?

Inès Lamunière: In fact, I've always been simultaneously both a teacher and a practitioner. Already as a student I was one of a generation who believed we had a role to play in defining the actual content of the education we were given, pushing for outside lecturers to be invited to the Architecture Department of the Ecole Polytechnique Fédérale de Lausanne [EPFL, Swiss Institute of Technology Lausanne] – theoreticians such as Manfredo Tafuri or Kenneth Frampton, or architect-theorists like Alan Colquhoun or Paolo Portoghesi. I've never been able to imagine doing architecture without at the same time assuming my responsibilities as an intellectual, engaged in ongoing debate on my own discipline. Hence my final-year project on the urban development of the Ostia-Fiumicino area of Rome, under the joint supervision of Joseph Rykwert and Paolo Portoghesi. The drawings I showed reflected ideas that were about urban development as much as architecture – that was the theoretical aspect. I preferred to express an architectural thought through drawing, not because I especially like it, but rather because, for me, architecture is first of all something that develops through drawing. Then came my residence at the Swiss Institute in Rome, where I met historians and practitioners of other disciplines – a very rich cultural environment.

Piccolo Porto
Giglio, 2017

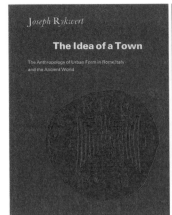

Kenneth Frampton
Modern Architecture: A Critical History, 1980

Joseph Rykwert
The Idea of a Town, 1976

Paolo Portoghesi
Le inibizioni dell'architettura moderna, 1974

12   On my return to Switzerland, I learnt German and joined the Swiss Institute of Technology Zurich [ETH] as an assistant, first to Franz Oswald, and then with Werner Oechslin for five years. Oechslin made me responsible for a time for his course on the baroque, which allowed me to take advantage of, and to further develop, the research I'd done in Rome on three of the most famous of baroque architects: Borromini, Cortona and Bernini. At the same time, but at the University of Geneva School of Architecture (where I also taught), Bruno Reichlin and Patrick Devanthéry were working on the modernist architectural heritage, notably in connection with a number of exhibitions celebrating the centenary of Le Corbusier's birth; research, for example, on the competition for the League of Nations headquarters, which would be published by ETH's Institute for the History and Theory of Architecture [gta]. One thing that has seemed to me to be essential, from the very start, and which I always try to communicate to my colleagues, as I do to my students and research assistants, is the idea that the project itself embodies theory. Because a great deal of what is usually called architectural theory is grounded in the choices an architect makes in the course of a project, the successive decisions that have to be taken. So theory isn't necessarily developed in writing, even if, during the twentieth century – though no doubt less often now – some of the most renowned architects did do that, and brilliantly.

Jean Baudrillard and Jean Nouvel
Les objets singuliers:
Architecture et philosophie, 2000

Philip Ursprung
Herzog & de Meuron:
Histoire naturelle, 2002

Rem Koolhaas
Conversations with Students, 1996

JML reflected in Maya Lin's
Vietnam Veterans Memorial
Washington D. C., 1982

So there are no boundaries between theory and practice, history
and project?
I think there is a theory proper to the project that is developed through
the realisation of the project. When, as an architect, you're engaged in an
assignment, you're faced with a series of choices, and you take the decisions that lead to the final outcome. In this sense, for the architect-creator,
a kind of theory emerges in the course of the process. There is no clear
boundary between the theory and practice. The realisation of the project
is another form of systematisation of thought that runs parallel to the
architect's own practice as a theorist, a role which, for me, is to historicise
theory and critique.

Was this dual career something that came naturally to your generation?
To return to the generation of students with whom I trained at EPFL in the
early 1980s, what I recall is that we were all capable of both conceiving
architectural projects and engaging with theoretical questions. We were
in constant discussion with sociologists, historians and philosophers,
notably through Faces – Journal d'architectures, established in Geneva
in 1985. In my years at EPFL, there were people like Bruno Marchand,
Patrick Devanthéry, Pierre-Alain Croset and Laurent Chenu, all of us very
open to the international exchange of ideas, with the English-speaking

Pick a spot in the city and begin to think of it as yours. It doesn't matter where, and it doesn't matter what. A street corner, a subway entrance, a tree in the park. Take on this place as your responsibility.

Sophie Calle and Paul Auster
Gotham Handbook, 1998

Sylvie Fleury
Eternity Now, Geneva, 2016

14 world and with Italy. But we were also keen to give lectures and be involved in exhibitions and publications. As researchers and activists, in 1987, we presented an exhibition in the Immeuble Clarté on Le Corbusier in Geneva from 1922 to 1932, which led to the authorities listing it as a historic monument. At the same time, the very intellectually demanding venture of *Faces*, whose editorial committee I joined in 1989, proved itself to be an invaluable channel for the circulation of ideas between the arts, architecture and urbanism. It was sometimes tiring to be both writing and teaching, but it was certainly fascinating and productive in terms of ideas for my own work as an architect.

To what extent did your family background contribute to this vocation? You seem to have been literally born into architecture.
I was indeed born into architecture; no question about it! It's something I say myself, like some others of my generation – Roger Diener, Oliver Schwarz, Valerio Olgiati, to mention only a few. From childhood on, I was immersed in a culture (in my case on account of my father's profession; for others, it was their mother's) that had a profound influence on me. I had the experience of architecture *in vivo*: an intellectual experience nourished by a wealth of discussions, travels, a certain open-minded curiosity – and I consider myself lucky for it. Although as a teenager, and then at different

Jørn Utzon
Bagsværd Church, Copenhagen, 1976

Louis I. Kahn
Franklin D. Roosevelt Four Freedoms Park, New York, 2012

times in my life, I had less personal contact with my father, Jean-Marc Lamunière, today, now that he's dead, I realise how much he taught me. I inherited his book collection, and even though I didn't keep everything, his library and mine were and are one – dedicated to keeping abreast of the times, remaining contemporary, yes, but also critical of the contemporary. This is witnessed by the annotations my father made in his books, very often first editions he acquired the moment they came out. A good number of critical works, too, which I would have read as well, each reflecting a certain theoretical moment. There's a lot that could be said about architects' libraries, especially when I think of Werner Oechslin's legendary, encyclopaedic one, where I spent so much time photographing originals: Borromini and Spada's *Opus Architectonicum*, a double page from an issue of *L'Esprit nouveau*… That said, what is important is first to go and see these architects' works *in vero*, rather than getting to know them from a monograph, however useful such things might be for teaching, in class or in the studio. My own personal approach to a building is always based on a visit. On the other hand, it's as important to me to understand what someone like William Curtis, Kenneth Frampton or Robert Venturi finds in the same building as it is to form my own opinion on direct contact with it.

**Ich frage mich als Architekt: «Die Magie des Realen»
– Cafe im Studentenwohnheim, ein Bild von Hans
Baumgartner, aus den dreißiger Jahren. Diese Männer
sitzen da und es gefällt ihnen. Ich frage mich: Kann ich
solche Atmosphären, kann ich diese Dichte, diese
Stimmung, kann ich als Architekt das entwerfen?**

Peter Zumthor
Atmosphären: Architektonische Umgebungen –
Die Dinge um mich herum, 2006

STUDIO

To teach is to take a stance. It is to formulate a proposition about
architecture.

Yes. That's a good definition. One thing in particular that has been important to me from the start, in teaching, is the notion that architecture is
a discipline in its own right that requires a whole series of things to be
mastered: it is a matter of acquiring instruments, notably geometry and
drawing, that enable the perception and comprehension of space, but
also other tools that are more cultural, historical or conceptual. And all
this without neglecting architecture's geographical, social and economic
context. Architecture has only a relative autonomy, as Pierre Bourdieu
would have said, but it nonetheless remains a distinct discipline whose
specificities, frames of reference and methods and resources must be
brought to students' understanding. A pretty traditional definition, in fact.

But project timescales being defined by the academic calendar and
school projects always remaining on paper, isn't teaching always a matter
of restricting yourself?

Yes, the semester system is always a determining factor. Over 14 weeks
it imposes a rhythm, a choreography of inputs intended to communicate
the knowledge on the basis of which each student develops his or her
own project. And for me, that also means attending very carefully to each

Christo
Valley Curtain, Rifle, Colorado, 1972

Jean Nouvel
Design for Tokyo Opera House, 1986

18   student's initial explorations – "I love beginnings", Louis Kahn would say – and prompting them to give form to their ideas. Teaching at master's level is a matter of enabling students to engage in a thought process that helps them coordinate their ideas in such a way as to further the development of their architectural language. In that respect, true, teaching is to restrict yourself, but means honing what you say, so as to enable the different projects to evolve more freely. What I am doing is not teaching a style or passing on particular formal affinities, but teaching a conceptual attitude in parallel with the processes involved in giving form to an idea.

    <u>To put the question another way: how do you seek, despite the limitations of the academic context, to achieve this holistic understanding of architecture that you advocate?</u>
I've always felt it necessary to back up the theme I set my students with a series of theory lectures which I very deliberately call "Theory of the Architectural Project". In these, I discuss the different ways of approaching a project that I have noted in other architects. This is intended to give my students a frame of reference, a set of exemplars in which I am simply one among others. Whether in the second year or on the master's, I always try and assemble a selection of architects or projects that can

Peter Zumthor
Kunsthaus Bregenz [KUB], 1997

Foster Associates
Willis Faber & Dumas Building, Ipswich, 1975

serve as key references, representing moments or situations that have 19
changed the course of architecture. How do you get students to recognise
such moments? And how then do you get them to understand that in their
own project work they are also engaging in this kind of operation? So
I very much like to give a lecture I call "Black Ghost/White Ghost", which
looks at the very precise historical moment that sees the emergence of
the problematic of the veiled building, as one might say. The moment
when architects began to "cover up" a lot of buildings, so as to give
them a distinctive formal presence in the urban space: the black form of
Jean Nouvel's model for the Tokyo Opera, and at the same time the milky
appearance of Peter Zumthor's Kunsthaus Bregenz, which seem to reso-
nate, as architecture, with work like Christo and Jeanne-Claude's. How
can the seemingly diametrically opposed choices of these two architects,
by virtue of their very power and force, spur other projects, inspire my
students? That's what I'm interested in, the so many "innovations" we
find in the history of architecture. So when, in 1927, Le Corbusier sets
the secretariat building of the Palais des Nations parallel to Lake Geneva
and detaches it from that of the Assembly, he effects a reinvention of the
"palace", which, from then on, owes nothing or almost nothing to the
Palace of Versailles.

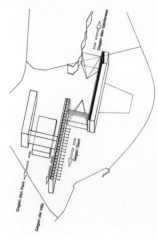

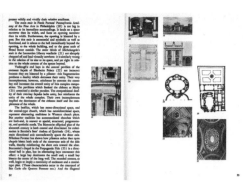

Inès Lamunière
and Patrick Devanthéry
Schematic representation of
the relationship of Le Corbusier's
League of Nations project to
the landscape, 1988

Le Corbusier and Pierre Jeanneret
League of Nation's project, Photomontage
showing proposed building in context, 1927

Robert Venturi
Complexity and Contradiction
in Architecture, 1966

20   An approach informed by history?
You have to be able to engage with history, particularly as it relates to
the project and to theory, which is why I advocate a holistic and engaged
approach. In *Complexity and Contradiction*, for example, Robert Venturi
uses critique to propose a way of seeing: the colour photographs marshalled
into the wonderful, landscape-format, double-page spreads of the second
edition suffuse the text with their presence, effecting an extraordinary –
combative – reordering of history. Siegfried Giedion, who believed one had
to be "imbued" with the history of one's own time in order to detect the
traces of the past, developed the idea of what he called a "dynamic history".
Giedion, Venturi… their persuasive force as teachers has always served
as an example in my own teaching. So for every document or building we
discuss, I always specify its historic sources, while retaining the freedom
to highlight different kinds of connections.

Among the influences you often refer to in your writings, Francesco
Borromini, Gian Lorenzo Bernini and Pietro da Cortona have twentieth-century
descendants in Le Corbusier, Robert Venturi, Jean Nouvel or Peter Zumthor.
It's a very specific, modernist genealogy of architects as plastic artists…
If I am as much enamoured of these three architects of the 1650s as I am of
Le Corbusier and Venturi in the twentieth century, it's because they're both

Giuseppe Vasi
Santa Maria della Pace, Rome, 1756

Pietro da Cortona
Santa Maria della Pace, Tempietto
Rome, 1657

Pietro da Cortona
Santa Maria della Pace, Piazzetta, Rome, 1657

Inès Lamunière and Patrick Devanthéry
Tempietto, Sketch made on site, 1983

modern and happy to take liberties with that modernity. Their drawings present an architecture that demands to be built, you might say. Yes, these architects are very much plastic artists, but in the contemporary sense. In the same way as I have at home a number of works of contemporary art chosen as much for their conceptual as for their formal aspect. They are as intelligent as they are beautiful!

Borromini's architecture can be described as conceptual first and foremost, but when set in context, constructed, it reshapes itself, folding into more intricate geometrical figures. Bernini explained, on his visit to Paris in 1665, that when carving a statue, a hand held away from the body had to be made larger in proportion in order to look right and convincing. If you look at Pietro da Cortona's design for Santa Maria della Pace – and he was indeed more of a painter than he was an architect – you see that it represents an almost pictorial *mise en scène*. The facades of the church and piazza unfurl in a series of folds on either side of a portico that takes the form of an antique *tempietto*, somewhat compressed. If you look at the drawings for it at the Albertina, you see that work on the plan proceeded extremely slowly, even just in determining the shape of the oval, which isn't quite oval, either. It is a very odd shape, in fact. That's what interests me, this way of constructing architecture, this practice of architecture, the fascinating complexity that I endeavour to bring out as a teacher, that

Edward Hopper
Eleven A.M., 1926

Georgia O'Keeffe
Pink Dish and Green Leaves, 1928

22 I seek to convey to my students, and which, in the end, I also hope to find in my own projects – those I undertake with the firm.

Does the academic framework allow the taking of liberties, the slowness you mention?
Yes, you simply have to grasp those liberties, know how to exercise them. An outline, fortunately, is no more than a kind of general orientation. Within that, students have to make choices: they have had the benefit, especially at EPFL, of a great diversity of teaching, which helps them make sense of their own – always personal – development as young architects. That's something I appreciate. It allows me to focus, in class and in the studio, on my own teaching on the urban-development project and its specificity as architecture.

How is the project studio organised?
At LAMU [Laboratory of Urban Architecture and Mobility], my staff and I function as a real team. From 8.30 in the morning, a certain work discipline rules, a discipline tempered by the pleasure of being together. Team spirit is enormously important. When we see each other later, after the students have left the school, or left the firm, where a lot of them go afterwards, we always end up talking about the collective aspect. As for me, with all

my years of experience behind me, I'm much quicker at working out what I want to do in the context of the project studio and I give more precise indications of what I'm after, which makes sense to my team and to the students. In recent years, we've been working on the topic of infrastructure and other public amenities, while also ensuring that students encounter urban scales with which we're unfamiliar in Switzerland. We've had to look to other cities, other lands, other environments, such as New York and Shanghai. Friends we've made there over the years help us get our bearings and suggest avenues of exploration. Confronting other milieus allows you to explore the ways in which an architectural project can offer a response to problems of infrastructure or public facilities. That response isn't always simple, hence our use of the term "risk-taking objects" to speak of constructions that obviously still fall within the ambit of architecture, but where the architecture can't be reduced to the creation of an isolated object. It's a question, then, of carefully defining the frame of reference on the basis of which you embark on the project proper. Supporting materials can be of all sorts: films, novels, demographic data, climatic information, planning documents, press cuttings, historical studies… Identifying the key features of the situation so as to then try and densify or develop the space based on an infrastructure that may be judged obsolete or, conversely, necessary – that's our goal. In parallel,

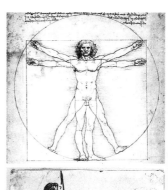

Stanley Kubrick
2001: A Space Odyssey, 1968

Leonardo da Vinci
The Vitruvian Man, c. 1490

Giovanni Battista Piranesi
Human figures, c. 1760

Roman Signer
Kabine, Swiss Pavilion
Venice Biennale, 1999

24   my team develops each semester a portrait-format A3 album, consisting of eight double-page spreads, that articulates the frame of reference within which the questions being tackled by the workshop will be developed, from the transport infrastructure to its effects on urbanisation and density.

What is striking in these albums is the frequent recurrence of certain themes that you designate by such keywords as "the contemporary city", "atmosphere", "green and grey", "sleep landscape", "work landscape", but also the lack of any information about the programme. Why this absence? Yes, each brochure calls for a description of the space – in the broader sense – where the project will unfold. Whether Shanghai, New York, Evian or Geneva, you highlight certain characteristic features of the city: population and demographic change, the local weather, key phases of urban development, milestones in its history, features of the urban culture, filmography, literature. It's a sort of compilation of objective data and more subjective impressions that helps identify the contextual aspects that make for its *genius loci*. This approach through fragments, open-ended and unfinished, is essential. The keywords are only a way of grouping things together in terms of the inputs that go into the making of the urban culture of that place, that city. On top of the investigative and, sometimes, somewhat speculative imaginary of the brochures comes a physical immersion in

Xu Zhen
In Just a Blink of an Eye
Basle, 2014

Jeffrey Shaw
Waterwalk, Amsterdam, 1969

Harold E. Edgerton
Densmore Shute Bends the Shaft, 1938

the selected city. So the experience of the field trip is crucial. It's then that the project site is grasped in the reality of its context. I organise meetings with architects and teachers who are active on the ground and engaged in the local debate. And finally, the trip also offers an opportunity to visit architects' offices and see how – in terms of organisation, project tools, technologies – they seek to meet the challenges presented by the great metropolises in which they operate.

I think the project can only be constructed on the basis of a reality perceived and understood in fragments. Each student must "construct" his or her reality, little by little. The same goes for the programme. I use keywords like "sleep landscape" to refer to a programme for non-permanent accommodation, whether hotel or residential, or "landscape of work" to cover the programme for offices and activities in shared spaces. This seems to me to be more appropriate than any reference to the functional typologies that emerged with modernism and which today are undergoing radical transformation.

How is the practical work of the project semester organised?
The course adopts a distinctive project methodology. In the first critique, the student is required to show two "pre-images" in A2 format. These particular drawings must present the articulation between a first, reasoned

Stanley Kubrick
2001: A Space Odyssey, 1968

Marco Ferreri
Ciao Maschio, 1978

Superstudio
Atti Fondamentali: Amore, (La macchina innamoratrice), 1972

26   conception and a certain idea of atmosphere. Characteristically exploratory, these images represent a first vision of what the building might be.
Nothing is yet known of its functionality or structure, but the imagery offers
an impressionistic account of its relationship to its environment, in terms
of both interior and exterior. It bears no relationship to a perspective view
or any conventional image, which is why I prefer the term "pre-image".
The project introduces atmospheres and formal and aesthetic themes in a
reinterpretation of its context. It's a matter of imagining what this building
might be, and what might be its environment. The pre-image, then, isn't
a perspective view, but a true drawing. Alongside this exploratory image
there will be a section and, sometimes, an axonometric projection as a
syntagmatic representation of the relationship between the urban, mobility and the different uses. The section, larger in scale, dominates the final
display, alongside the pre-images.

Some images or key descriptions appear in every project outline,
whatever the city selected, among them Kubrick's *2001: A Space Odyssey*,
Kollhoff's Atlanpole, Koolhaas's *Lagos*, Murakami's description of the city
as an organism.
Yes, it's always this idea of establishing a frame of reference that I try to
get across to them, in terms of contemporary and, more particularly, urban

Joel Sternfeld
Looking South on a May Evening
(the Starrett-Lehigh Building), New York City, 2000

Chris Blaser
Eau douce, Léman, 2006

Leo Fabrizio
Alpage de Nervaux, 2005

culture. The framework is always mine, to some degree, but the students have to learn to create their own. And there's always one nagging question: what is "the spirit of the age"; from what elements does it derive?

In the brochure, there's also always the photo of Jenny Holzer's projection on the Arno embankment in Florence, *I Smell You On My Skin*. The city speaks to us emotionally; it's not just an advertising medium. There's also Martin Kippenberger's work with his *Metro-Net* transportable subway entrances in Kassel, which deals with infrastructure, the subterranean. As for *2001: A Space Odyssey*, it's a film that remains enigmatic, although, paradoxically, it can be stimulating not to understand everything! But there is an atmosphere, this man's presence in space, in the geometry of the fuselage and in that strange apartment where you hear nothing but his breathing… In this film, at the end, there is also the appearance of the black monolith, silent and beautiful, which has always made me think of Mies van der Rohe's Seagram Building. Archetype, prototype or sculpture?

This imaginary museum is always complemented by images of your own work. What is their role?
Projects I have been able to build I can use to illustrate certain themes. The realisation of the RTS tower in Geneva thus offers an opportunity to discuss the idea of modifying a hieratic form (the tower) to create an

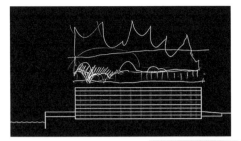

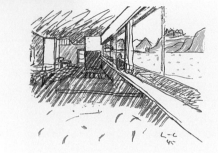

Herzog & de Meuron
Sketch of the Elbphilharmonie in Hamburg, 2003

Le Corbusier
Une petite maison, 1954 (1945)

Ann Veronica Janssens
L'ODRRE N'A PAS D'IPMROTNCAE
Geneva, 2012

28 emblematic building that is more "misshapen" (the periscope); making it possible to shift from the agglomeration and stacking of individual work cells to freeing up extensive work areas linked by atria. A building integrated into the urban context – a gleaming, mirrored edifice whose dynamic visual effects discreetly suggest the moving image, television and the digital.

The publications that result from the semester projects, on the other hand, are illustrated with photographs by Leo Fabrizio. Isn't that a return to a "superficial" representation in the sense that these photographs represent only the surface of the space?
Photographers are good companions – tough sometimes, but enormously valuable. I often have a theme that is distinct from any building or object that could be photographically documented. In *Habiter la menace* [Living with Danger], for instance, it was necessary to give some account of the variety of structures found in Switzerland to protect against natural hazards. How could we make it clear that these installations, common as they are, are most often camouflaged so as not to arouse fear, or at least a certain anxiety? To deal with this topic, it was important to go in search of these sites and the particular atmosphere they generate. Leo Fabrizio went off on a reportage and returned with photographs that went

Leo Fabrizio
Aire de Charrat, en direction de Sion, 2014

Alvaro Siza
Swimming-pool at Leça da Palmeira, Porto, 1973

Le Corbusier
Unité d'habitation, Marseille, 1952

far beyond book illustrations in their character as art and their aesthetic impact in large format. Two years ago, he gave a different twist to the same approach for *Objets risqués* [Risk-taking Objects]. What I love in his work is that he shows us something that can only be seen if you give yourself the time to hunt for it, searching for it through the lens. His photographs represent the real, but a real that offers us hints, that suggests the possible site of a project.

You've taught for more than 20 years, first at ETH in Zurich and then at EPFL in Lausanne. Over this period, it seems to me that your approach to architecture has developed from a critical conception of the discipline in the 1990s to more pragmatic and perhaps more optimistic responses over recent years. Has this shift been reflected in your teaching?

Yes, definitely. There were two key moments, the first being my experiences at Harvard, in the United States, in 1996 and 1999, which prompted me to rethink my teaching at Lausanne. Then was the development of architectural research at EPFL under the presidency of Patrick Aebischer, which enabled me to gain my freedom and to engage with contemporary issues. It also allowed me to take more pleasure in teaching, without constantly asking myself whether what I was doing was right, or suitable to the level of my students. Having been made a professor very young,

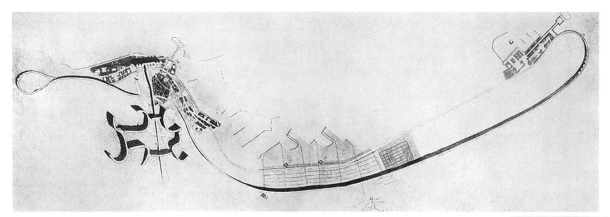

Le Corbusier
Plan Obus, Project A, Algiers, 1931

Anselm Kiefer
Studio complex at Barjac, 1993–2009

30 I had always tried to be as exhaustive and systematic as possible, always wanting to get it right, to miss nothing out, to the point of setting aside my own interests. At Harvard, I was supposed to represent the "Swiss" qualities that Rafael Moneo and then Jorge Silvetti wanted to promote at the school: an interest in construction, perfection of detail, sensitivity to materials, an understanding of the object as a generator of emotion. That was the strength of my contribution, but also its limitation, as I discovered on meeting teachers from the English-speaking world, or from Latin America. It was then that I started to question the architecture of the individual object, becoming more interested in architecture as contributor to the urban. So that's when I became interested in the question of the "large scale", conceiving for the first time a long-term programme of research that is still going on today, as it happens. In 2006 and 2007, health problems stopped me working altogether. But in 2008, re-energised by the break, I went back to teach at Harvard then, on returning to Lausanne, I continued along the same lines with work on the relationships between transport infrastructure and urban development. On brownfield railway land, first of all, then with the Complex Design doctoral programme, through which I supervised several doctoral theses. Essentially, I'd say, my teaching falls into three periods: pre-Harvard, post-Harvard and what I've been doing over the last ten years.

Et presque tout de suite je la reconnus, c'était Venise, dont mes efforts pour la décrire et les prétendus instantanés pris par ma mémoire ne m'avaient jamais rien dit et que la sensation que j'avais ressentie jadis sur deux dalles inégales du baptistère de Saint-Marc m'avait rendue avec toutes les autres sensations jointes ce jour-là à cette sensation-là, et qui étaient restées dans l'attente, à leur rang, d'où un brusque hasard les avait impérieusement fait sortir, dans la série des jours oubliés.

Marcel Proust
A la recherche du temps perdu, vol. 7: Le Temps retrouvé, 1927

Le Corbusier
Model for Plan Obus, Algiers, 1931

Chaque pierre était l'étrange concrétion d'une volonté, d'une mémoire, parfois d'un défi. Chaque édifice était le plan d'un songe.

Marguerite Yourcenar
Mémoires d'Hadrien, 1951

WORDS

In one of your project outlines you introduce the term *"ville-monde"*, the idea of the city as world. From Alberti to Aldo van Eyck, people have more commonly spoken of the city as house. Does the city as world signify a change of scale or even a change of paradigm in contemporary architectural practice?

I had the good fortune to study under the sociologist Michel Bassand and the historian André Corboz. Metropolisation, the city as structured environment. The shift from city as surface area to the city as network. They were the people who really made me question Alberti's notion of the city as a big house and the palace as a small city. But the idea of the *"ville-maison"* itself is lovely. It's like *Femme Maison*, that wonderful drawing by Louise Bourgeois. The intimacy, the form, the essential house. That's something that's always fascinated me, the triangle atop a square. The slightly clumsy hand-drawn picture that becomes architecture. If I had to draw the city, it would have something of those drawings of triangles perched on squares, their lovely silhouette.

The city as house, I think, represents a way of thinking very different from the city as world. The city as world is, first of all, a radical change of scale, of course. It is also a complex distributional system of transport and access that connects people via new temporalities. Non-places, link-places: there, architecture is no longer a matter of perspective construction in the

Citadel wall
Hué, 2013

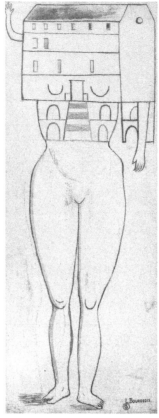

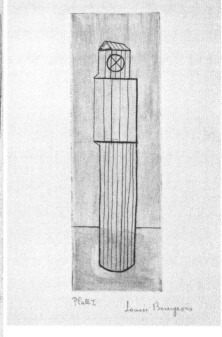

Pablo Picasso
Femme aux bras écartés, Detail, 1962

Louise Bourgeois
Femme-Maison, 1946–1947

Louise Bourgeois
Plate 1, 1947

34 classical manner; it is no longer the "great theatre" in which the social is continually represented or represents itself. Nor is it the beautiful collection of sculptural objects the modernists dreamt of. The city as world is a perturbation; it is experienced in fragments. For architecture, then, it's a question of modifying something, rather than just building in an empty space. That's what interests me in the city as world.

This idea of the city as world is central to architecture today. You see fragments of it built or in the building: Jean Nouvel's design for the Louvre Abu Dhabi is in many ways an outstanding example. A lot has been said about the internationalisation of the 1950s. But here, faced with the elaboration of new cultural models, Nouvel asks whether there might not be an architecture that might prove itself "universal". His building is conceived for that place and that climate, but the Louvre Abu Dhabi is also a universal museum of civilisations and their relationship to art. It is conceived both as a great palace and as a small world. It brings together museum collections and transposes them to a new palace by translating the scale and the notion of rooms and the courtyard.

I think too of a Herzog & de Meuron project currently in the course of construction, their M+ in Hong Kong. The building takes the form of an inverted T set above the transport infrastructure of the Airport Express railway. There too, the programme of the museum and the architecture

Siegfried Giedion
Rockefeller Center, Photomontage, 1941

Lee Friedlander
New Orleans, 1969

of the building are addressed to a broad, transcultural public, while still being rooted in the particular context of Hong Kong. In its scale, its sense of being a sign, a poster for itself on the skyline, it draws on the idea of the illuminated sign while reinventing it on an entirely new scale. The brilliance of the Elbphilharmonie in Hamburg likewise lies in this very particular appropriation of the built context, which literally becomes the base, the architectural-scale plinth to a work of plastic art. In the hands of Nouvel or Herzog & de Meuron, these great containers for art and culture are contextualised – and that's what may seem paradoxical – to become more universal.

The themes you choose, such as mobility, infrastructure, urban development or communications, are key problems in today's world, but they're problems over which, paradoxically, architects seem to have lost any form of control. They bring into play new actors and call for skills or new technologies that appear to fall outside the domain of architecture as it has been understood, for the most part, by the theory of classical architecture to which you refer. How then can they be addressed?

The relationship between mobility, infrastructure, urban development and space was the subject of "Avenir des aires ferroviaires en Suisse" [The Future of Railway Land in Switzerland] between 2005 and 2009, the first of my research projects to be funded by the Swiss National Science

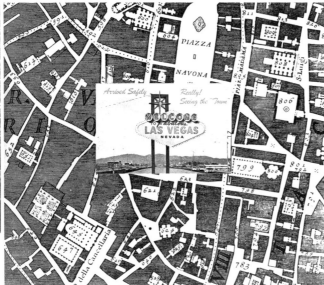

Giovanni Battista Piranesi
Campo Marzio dell'Antica
Roma, 1762

Robert Venturi, Denise Scott Brown and Steven Izenour
Nolli's Map of Rome (detail), 1972

OMA/Rem Koolhaas and Bruce Mau
What Ever Happened to Urbanism?, 1995

36 Foundation. Aside from my almost romantic fascination with trains, railway stations and the public spaces associated with them, I realised that contemporary mobility confronted us with fundamental questions about our way of life. Mobility and the transport that made it possible were for a long time thought of as something wonderful, and railway terminals were like public cathedrals. And then, suddenly, at the turn of the new millennium, it became clear that these systems had grown obsolete and that we needed to think about these vast, abandoned expanses. These were different from the industrial fringes we'd had to deal with in the 1990s and which had so exercised the architectural imagination. A great deal of imagination, and a great deal of work too! These brownfield railway lands extended over thousands of square metres right in the city centres, seemingly inhospitable sites that could accommodate new urban developments, the growth of the city. Simultaneously, public-transport authorities began to scent possible profits, and restructured themselves, separating their activities into different divisions: transport, infrastructure, property. Of all the disciplines that had something useful to say about the future of this disused land, it was sociology that struck me as being the key, so we set up a joint research team with Vincent Kaufman and his Urban Sociology Laboratory at EPFL. It was essential to understand the new forms of mobility and what might be the future of this surplus land no longer required by

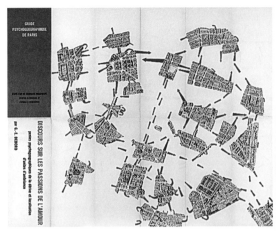

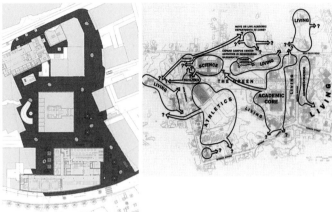

Guy Debord
Guide psychogéographique de Paris:
Discours sur les passions de l'amour, 1957

Pipilotti Rist
and Carlos Martinez
Stadtlounge, St Gallen, 2005

Venturi Scott Brown & Associates (VSBA)
Area planning study for Bryn Mawr College (near Philadelphia), 1997

the railways. From what we called "pioneering appropriations" (alternative activities, squatted premises, etc.) to projects motivated by ever-growing financial pressures, what assistance could be offered to those involved in such projects, whether voluntary groups or local authorities, or indeed public bodies as powerful as the Swiss Federal Railways? We were able to make numerous recommendations regarding the importance of mixed use, types of funding and the architectural typologies and urban forms that were called for.

To brownfield railway sites must be added those appropriated for road transport, remarkably evoked in Ursula Meier's wonderful film *Home*. In the books I came across as a child, on modern spatial planning, I thought the motorways were wonderful and the viaducts above Château de Chillon absolutely superb. They still are, but today they entertain a very different relationship to the landscape, which is a largely urbanised and more heterogeneous environment. Now there was a theme for research, for a project that engaged with the spirit of the age. Not just in terms of form, but because it called for reflection on the environment in the wider sense. Mobility seemed to me to offer a way of thinking about space on a larger scale, in other words to rethink the relationships between space, urbanism and architecture. As we know, this mobility was, for the most part, left in the hands of engineers trained in schools that since the nineteenth century

Jeff Wall
The Storyteller, 1986

Maglev train
Shanghai, 2016

Ursula Meier
Home, 2008

Jean-Frédéric Schnyder
Walking-Tour, 1993

38 had had less and less to do with architecture; a separation that throughout the twentieth century would prompt tensions, but also a mutual fascination, between architects and engineers.

These themes were also inspired by my professional practice, by the processes that I was developing in the context of integrated contracts. Something that needed to be done there was to establish a dialogue with engineers to put issues of spatiality, use and culture back into the problematic of mobility. This year, the contract for a new subterranean station in Geneva, to be built beneath the existing Cornavin railway station, was won by Interfaces, a team in which my firm is a partner. The question there is to ensure the success of the transition between the circulation spaces underground and the urban spaces at street level, and, in burying the extension beneath the ground, to create an enhanced central public space for the city.

How can you teach students this kind of collaboration?
I try and communicate what I know; to systematise that knowledge with the help of a small group of experts who have gradually come to specialise on the subject. I'm thinking of the engineer Yves Bach, who's brilliant on questions of infrastructure, underground construction and so on. Or Aurelio Muttoni, for questions of towers – because for me a tower is an

Gordon Matta-Clark
Day's End (Pier 52), 1975

Pipilotti Rist
Nothing
Venice Biennale, 1999

Roman Signer
Kabine, Swiss Pavilion
Venice Biennale, 1999

infrastructure, not a building. The sociological aspect is generally covered 39 by Vincent Kaufman and Luca Pattaroni, who perpetuate the legacy of Michel Bassand, responsible for introducing sociology to EPFL.

And what is the role of technology?

Technology is central, because today it occupies more than a third of a building; the things that make it habitable are practically as important as the space actually inhabited. Students have to understand that. They have to develop specific project strategies in which what used to be the poché contains a multitude of things. For example, for tackling very large-scale projects, following the thinking of Ernst Neufert or of Rem Koolhaas at the Venice Biennale of 2014 in their focus on elements, I suggest a kind of dimensional primer, a schedule of standard dimensions for spans, slab thickness, staircases, lifts, ducts, false ceilings, false floors, platforms, tracks and so on. These are the basic invariants constitutive of the distinctive metrics of large-scale projects, which they are able to learn and make use of.

Buildings like railway stations are no more than nodes in a wider network. Why this interest in the station, rather than the connecting lines that more profoundly shape the space?

40 True, I am very interested in railway stations. They have to resolve the complex relation between modal interchange, infrastructure and development. In scale, they still fall within the domain of architecture.

This interest in architecture and in the object is reflected in other recurrent themes, such as that of atmosphere. What is the role of that in the project?

It is a complex issue, in that it's a question of conferring on an individual gesture a more general significance. In fact, I remain convinced that architecture has in some sense to constitute a shared experience, even if the aesthetic emotion "*à la Corbu*" that we learnt about as students, or, at the other extreme, the supposedly theoretically grounded "sign" of the semiologists, for a long time left us unsatisfied. No doubt the idea of atmosphere allows us to give a more architectural response to the question.

Architecture has created its own tools, in order to communicate, or, as I would rather say, to denote contents – in the case of classical architecture, the employment and selection of orders; in twentieth-century modernist architecture, the use of transparency; and for postmodernists, semantics, the sign. The professional generation of the 1990s, to which I belong, found that new emotional connections could be created through the choice of materials, the expression of a specific materiality of the object and its

Le Corbusier
Venice, Carnet La Roche, c. 1922

SANAA
Learning Center, EPFL, 2004

contents. Materials – concrete, or steel, for example – are to be thought of as "matter of art", in the fine phrase coined by my colleague Jacques Lucan. The "*Forme forte*" or "strong form" thus acquires a surface, an envelope, a veil. So concrete is dyed and metal anodised or oxidised. This is still very important to me today. In fact, the world of image and immediacy raises even more questions about the physical qualities of architecture. But it's not enough: the physical experience of architecture *in situ* calls, in addition, for a subtle mastery of the relations between exterior and interior spaces, between public and more private spaces, between spaces of circulation and spaces of rest. Architecture has to offer an experience. A particularly complex interplay between what it houses and what it communicates. It's very difficult today to articulate the transition between private space that belongs only to you and shared space that is part of the public realm and thus a wider culture more generally, which must be taken into account.

I often say to my students that I love "elegant" buildings, but I think it is Herzog & de Meuron and Jean Nouvel in particular who have offered us the experience of this elegance, as much in intellectual as in sensual terms. When I'm at the CaixaForum in Madrid, under that mass of brick and iron, in that kaleidoscopic space of stainless steel, there's something that goes beyond intelligence of concept and materials. This is architecture, not design! Just like the Schaulager in Basle, which I really love. These are

Ludwig Mies van der Rohe
Resor House, Collage with Paul Klee's
Colourful Meal (1928), 1939

Snøhetta
Norwegian Wild Reindeer Pavilion
Hjerkinn, 2011

42 buildings characterised by a certain austerity, but which emanate a luxury quite unafraid of itself. It's really very beautiful!

How can you give expression to this, how can you test for this special atmosphere in the context of the project?
It's a question of perception, and we come back to the pre-image I ask my students to produce. I ask them, "Do you like this building?" That might seem superficial, but not to my mind. Not so long ago, no one dared say, "That's beautiful".

And how do you create this atmosphere? The philosopher and sociologist Georg Simmel described "*Stimmung*" or mood as a question of framing, revealing the distinctive character of a landscape that would otherwise not be visible.
Yes, bringing out…

Well, all framing is linked to perspective…
…classical perspective is too reductive, in that it imposes a point of view. Now, however, the density of the city, the character of urban life, the simultaneity of different environmental sensations requires that we rethink both our perception of the real and its representation. So I'd love to be able

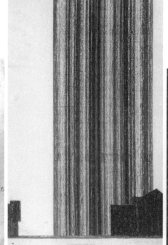

Hans Richter and Werner Gräff
Cover of G — Material
zur elementaren Gestaltung
no. 3, 1924

Ludwig Mies van der Rohe
Glass Skyscraper Project, 1922

Ludwig Mies van der Rohe
Friedrichstrasse Skyscraper
Project, 1921

to work with a moving image that would be both tactile and odoriferous. 43
For example, I remember the day when I visited the Belgian Pavilion at
the Venice Biennale of 1999. The artist Ann Veronica Janssens had filled
the space with a dense, whitish fog that brought about a destabilisation
of perception, of empty space itself, of the physical elements such as
walls and partitions and of the presence of other visitors. The distinctive
atmosphere this generated expressed a new physical and sensual relation
between body and space.

"Atmosphere" is an intrinsically vague notion. Atmosphere begins
where the building stops…
No, that's too reductive. I think a project of today has to be able to capture
in its geometry not only the physical elements and the light, but also the
other more immaterial elements that make such a contribution to the
wellbeing of the user: ventilation, climate control, acoustics, texture and
so on. Architects today have also to work with these factors, which can't
be reduced to their merely technical aspects. I tell my students that this
is the "construction" of sensation. Well, the tools required to communicate such an architecture have to go far beyond perspective. The age of
great perspective views such as were produced by Fabio Reinhart and his
assistant Miroslav Šik is past. Yes, of course, these views are still strong,

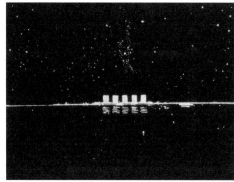

Ludwig Mies van der Rohe
Skyscraper Project, 1922

Le Corbusier
Précisions sur un état présent de l'architecture et de l'urbanisme, 1930

44   as images, some of them poetic, but the way of thinking, the analogic,
that governed their elaboration is obsolete.

<u>So what is it exactly, this pre-image that you teach your students?</u>
It's a matter of pre-visualising the architecture that will slowly but steadily
emerge through the use of the more traditional project tools. A pre-image
is a kind of vision – impressionistic, atmospheric.

<u>What does it consist of?</u>
It's an image that's presented. It's discussed during critiques, at the start
and during the course of the project. Its sets the theme for the primary emotional relationships established between context and architectural form,
interior and exterior. Sometimes a skyline, it might recall eighteenth-
century *vedute* for Venice; sometimes a *mise en scène*, a stage setting,
suggesting Claude Monet's urban landscapes of the Gare Saint-Lazare;
or, more recently, representations of twentieth-century urban space, like
Lee Friedlander's photographs in a rear-view mirror or Siegfried Giedion's
photographic fragments for the Rockefeller Center. In modernist days,
I think the showcase example might be Mies van der Rohe's masterly
visualisations for the Friedrichstrasse. Extraordinary perspective views
– large-format boards, the poster with the red G for the magazine of

Robert Venturi, Denise Scott Brown
and Steven Izenour
Learning from Las Vegas, 1972

Robert Venturi, Denise Scott Brown
and Steven Izenour
Physiognomy of a typical
casino sign, 1972

that title. Later Venturi's photographic assemblages for *Learning from Las Vegas*, or the Pop lyricism of Superstudio. All these images have something in common: they belong to the domain of art, and present themselves as such.

In my class on the pre-image, I always begin with Piranesi's imaginary palaces and prisons. From these there are two lessons to be learnt: I show them, as Ulya Vogt-Göknil used to do, that it's impossible to reconstruct the plan from these views. The perspective view conveys no truth about a plan. The other is the presence of figures, their silhouette and their scale. That immediately gives you a measure of monumentality. Sometimes I take my pencil and insert a figure into a student's drawing, larger or smaller as it might be, so important do I consider the choice of scale to be, and that from the very start of the project.

Another group of keywords draws on the idea of disaster, among them the *objet risqué* [the risk-taking object] and *habiter la menace* [living with danger]. What's a risk-taking object, exactly?

Behind the programmes of such objects are audacious approaches that have gambled, often against the odds; taking on board, rather than hiding from the more problematic aspects; relating to the context, rather than abstracting from it; innovating, rather than reproducing standard solutions.

El Croquis no. 53
OMA / Rem Koolhaas 1987/1992, 1992

OMA / Rem Koolhaas
Zeebrugge Sea Terminal, 1988

46 I often say that Geneva's Jet d'Eau fountain is one of the most magnificent risk-taking objects I know. The result of an integrated process bringing together engineering, geography and semantics, it transcends the status of mere solution to become iconic. The concept also covers architectural objects in the hazardous contexts – health-threatening contexts, say – that are today governed by standards of safety, air quality, noise, etc. Objects located close to railways, motorways, airports, or close to energy transport infrastructure or industrial zones, for example.

And what do you mean by "living with danger"?
"Living with danger" is about objects whose projects deal with these same questions, but in the context of protective works often located on so-called "natural" sites. Hydrological dangers, the threat of landslide or avalanche, or the proximity of ionising radiation. These raise questions about the very idea of a site. It's not a question of site as most often understood in architecture, neither the blank space of the modernist gaze, nor the abode of a *genius loci* whose character is largely derived from the memory of place and its customs (the space as palimpsest dear to André Corboz or Pierre Lavedan). Nowadays, you have to reverse that and analyse transformations of the built environment, not in terms of constraints or defects, but in the trickier terms of threat or risk.

Through the eyes of a high-flying night bird, we take in the scene from midair. In our broad sweep, the city looks like a single gigantic creature – or more like a single collective entity created by many intertwining organisms. [...] To the rhythm of its pulsing, all parts of the body flicker and flare up and squirm.

Haruki Murakami
After Dark, 2004

In establishing a relationship to a site considered inhospitable, you have to work differently: with other professions, with other social and economic stakeholders whom you are not generally in the habit of consulting, and on a scale where the unit of measure is not the human body but the car or the train. To confront students with these realities is to confront them, and all of us, with the need to innovate.

…with extreme realities that at the same time go to the very nature of architecture understood as shelter, as a place of protection…
Yes, in teaching I've always thought that it is in confronting complexity that you learn the most. What's more, when I was director of the architecture department, it was this idea that guided me in developing a scheme for teaching the architectural project that approaches complexity by theme, rather than by stages. A first year entirely devoted to architecture as a science of space: geometry, scale, circulation, representation and communication, architectural tools. A second year focused on architecture as fabrication: gravity, loadbearing, structure, material, system as integration versus juxtaposition. A third year looking at usage, at architecture as a mode for organising the way we live: types and classes of activities, of use. Then a two-year master's programme concentrating on urban development, density, mix of use and large-scale projects, simultaneously on frag-

Giovanni Battista Piranesi
The Gothic Arch, from the series Imaginary Prisons, 1761

48   ments of city and architectural objects (the "risk-taking objects"). An ideal syllabus that would lead on to doctoral studies in Complex Design. While I did indeed succeed in establishing the Complex Design programme, my plan for a new syllabus was fiercely criticised by my colleagues and never adopted.

     "Atmosphere", "danger", "risk" – these all have to do with transient states. On the other hand, there's another idea that's very important in your writing: that of "permanence". How does that relate to those themes we've just talked about?

We have to think architecture, like space, in all its different temporalities, which can extend from instantaneity to permanence. The question of permanence interests me especially on account of problems of obsolescence…the obsolescence of infrastructure, of the built environment, and, indeed, of some of the aspects of the way we live. Today we build in a built environment whose obsolescence sometimes represents the possibility of a project. Reformulations that embrace the "remains" of a built heritage that is often dilapidated, but sometimes still sturdy enough. Two of my students, for example, proposed a reconstruction of the railway station on the Rochers de Naye above Montreux, together with its site – a site that is glacial in winter, but only a brief train ride from the Montreux

...une unité linguistique est comparable à une partie d'un édifice, une colonne par exemple...

Ferdinand de Saussure
Cours de linguistique générale, 1906-1911

Giovanni Battista Piranesi
View of the Stone Pavement of the Appian Way
from the series Antichità Romane, 1756

Riviera and its palm trees. Their project is both a station and an emblematic, circular form; a form designed to associate urban pleasures and outdoor activities.

Fiona Pià's thesis on ski resorts considers the question of the urbanisation of the mountains at a time when the idea is increasingly rejected by the Swiss. It is a rejection evidenced by the success of the Lex Weber [legislation introduced by referendum banning the construction of holiday homes in areas where they represent more than 20 per cent of the housing stock] in 2012, and then the revision of spatial planning legislation a year later. Her research explores both the obsolescence and the dysfunctionality of recent patterns of urbanisation – together with the paradigm changes now underway – around environmental questions, natural hazards, the increase of sedentary, urban cultural activities in mountain resorts, etc. New questions arise, and with them new architectural possibilities. The architectural project can seek to respond to all this. Through the redefinition of scales, the mix of uses and the sizing of developments, architecture can take account of a much broader landscape, a different space. These new forms are eloquently expressive, fitting into an already largely built environment, in which they can play an emblematic role as new kinds of signs, one that is more complex and suggestive.

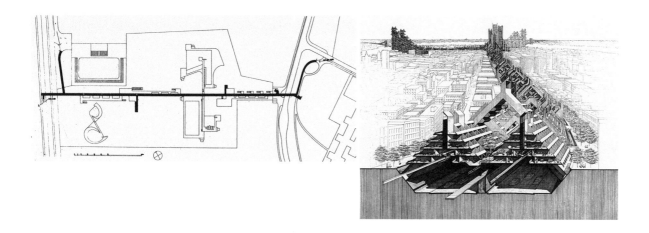

Aurelio Galfetti, Flora Ruchat-Roncati and Ivo Trümpy
Public baths, Bellinzona, 1967–1970

Paul Rudolph
City Corridor project for the Lower
Manhattan Expressway, 1967–1972

50   **Infrastructure is characterised not only by permanence but also by an efficiency tied to its mono-functionality.**

In the near future, tunnels, viaducts and other structures serving a mobility understood exclusively in terms of one type of transport may well turn out to be a new kind of wasteland... what I call mobility wasteland. Your remark is all the more pertinent given that neither symbolically nor physically are these structures anchored in a more complex geography concerned as much with urban development as with topography. A viaduct conceived for road transport could, in future, be integrated into other forms of mobility... or even give rise to other forms of urban development. In a territory as undulating and mountainous as Switzerland's, the horizontal line characteristic of mobility infrastructure is fertile with possibilities.

And what, finally, is "complex design", another term to which you seem to attach great importance?

When these questions of scale became important to me in my thinking on urban development, densification and land use, I felt it was important to address, to respond to, the question of scale, of the large scale, notably in establishing a new relationship – different from that espoused by modernism – between ideas like prefabrication, repetition and economy

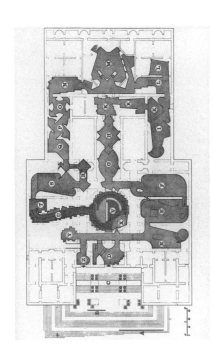

Dans ma ville sont présentes bien d'autres villes, par toutes sorte de médiations : les pancartes indicatrices, les manuels de géographie, les objets qui en viennent, les journaux qui en parlent, les images, les films qui me les montrent, les souvenirs que j'en ai, les romans qui me les font découvrir.

Michel Butor
Essais sur le roman, 1964

Paolo Portoghesi
Plan for the exhibition Michelangiolo architetto
Palazzo delle Esposizione, Rome, 1963

of construction. The critique of large-scale development that emerged in response to those early conceptions – in the work of sociologists or journalists like Jane Jacobs or Ada Louise Huxtable – led to various attempts to fragment and recompose the space in terms of smaller units, moving from all-embracing large-scale operations to a multiplicity of operations on a scale hopefully better managed. For my part, I felt it was essential to concentrate on the responses that architecture could offer, as a discipline, to programmes in the region of 100,000 m². The notion of "complex design" covers the kinds of architectural project and the specific strategies we need to develop for such built structures…

… that go beyond the scale of the architectural object…

Yes. We have to rethink the large forms at the intersection of architecture and urbanism – in the light, for instance, of Rem Koolhaas's "X" and "XL", or Hans Kollhoff's plans for Berlin's Moabit in the 1990s, or even some later built projects along the same lines, notably MVRDV's fairly astonishing contribution in the 2000s, and BIG's work today. But there are, of course, limits to the enlargement of architectural forms to such a scale, especially when the project is to be integrated into somewhat more complicated contexts, already urbanised and already as dense as railway stations and other mobility infrastructure. The interdisciplinarity of complex design has

Hugh Ferriss
The Metropolis of Tomorrow
Evolution of the Set-back Building
First Stage, 1922

Hans Kollhoff
Völkerkundmuseum, Frankfurt am Main, 1987

52   to take in law and economics. Input from these two disciplines is absolutely crucial when it comes to complicated, large-scale projects. Two colleagues in particular have supported me in developing this approach: Jacques Dubey at the EPFL and the University of Fribourg in matters of law, and Olivier Crevoisier of the University of Neuchâtel for real-estate economics. It's with them that we developed the Complex Design programme, a doctoral programme supported by the Swiss National Science Foundation, our goal being to teach architects and also economists and lawyers to engage in the cross-disciplinary dialogue necessary for the realisation of large-scale projects – complex undertakings not only on account of their scale, but also in the mix of uses and the great number of stakeholders involved, in terms of both politics and real-estate development.

Since the mid-2000s – looking, for example, at Herzog & de Meuron's Hamburg Philharmonie, OMA/Rem Koolhaas's Entrepôt Macdonald in Paris, or the redevelopment of the Alpine resort of Andermatt by Orascom – I note that all such projects have encountered serious problems in their execution. Magnificent they may be, but they have taken ten, 15 years, sometimes longer to complete, so many pitfalls were there on the way, and also, no doubt, because the necessary know-how (including the specific know-how of interdisciplinary collaboration) had not yet been sufficiently developed and tested. I've seen it in teaching the master's course:

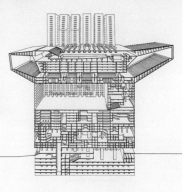

Paul Virilio
Bunker archéologie, Observation post revealed
by the erosion of the dunes, 1975

Jean Nouvel
Le Monolithe, Expo. 02, Morat, 2002

Hans Kollhoff
Project for Atlanpole, Nantes, 1988

to sensitise architects, to make them aware of the concerns that come 53
with large scale so they realise what scale is appropriate in considering
not only built structures and their installations, but also uses and func-
tions, calls for a next step.

These projects tend to fall outside the city, in relatively un-urbanised
zones…
They centre, I would say, on the artificial character of nature today. This
is a dangerous nature; it's not nature the way people used to think of
it, as something to be contemplated like a painting. Nature is changing
radically: mudslides, avalanches, tidal waves… I'm working, for example,
on a development on the banks of the Arve in Geneva that poses, from
the very start, the question of how you live alongside a turbulent river
that sometimes floods. That's the reality of nature for me, the angle from
which I approach it.

…je crains, si nous voulons des objets singuliers,
qu'il nous faille user des moyens de l'analyse,
de la réflexion, de la connotation, qu'il soit nécessaire
d'établir des relations entre des objectifs contradictoires,
bref qu'il soit indispensable de penser…

Jean Nouvel in Jean Baudrillard and Jean Nouvel
Les objets singuliers: Architecture et philosophie, 2000

LABORATORY

You have always combined practice with research.

For years, though, I couldn't find the quite right answer to the question of research in the university context. When I was a young teacher, at ETH in Zurich, the Department of Architecture organised a three-day symposium on the subject of research. It was at the Ittingen Charterhouse. The discussions were very unfocused. My own research was concerned with the project as process, using the archives newly classified and made available, notably at ETH's Institute for the History and Theory of Architecture, the Archives de la Construction Moderne at EPFL and the Fondation Le Corbusier.

I witnessed discussions between, on the one hand, the historians who wanted to reduce architectural theory to architectural history, or architectural history to architectural theory, and on the other, the specialists in architectural technology enthused by the idea that new 3D tools were going to influence the modes of production and understanding of space. Then there were architect colleagues like Flora Ruchat-Roncati and Hans Kollhoff, who had demonstrated in their practice how the project could – and should – be a source of knowledge. Hans Kollhoff, who made explicit reference to Oswald Mathias Ungers, had shown that this kind of research was neither new, nor special, but integral to all architectural activity.

55

Plaster prepared for
pantographic enlargement
Venice, 2015

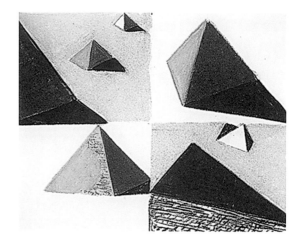

Erik Gunnar Asplund
Skogskyrkogården Tallum Pavilion
Stockholm, 1924

Louis I. Kahn
Study for a Mural Based on Egyptian Motifs
No. 1, 1951

56   I still think today that research focused on the body of materials generated by the project, on its process, is without question a valid form of scholarly endeavour. But at the time I had to do my research in critiquing projects, compiling dossiers or writing feature articles for different journals or collective works. Countless articles, addressing the questions that interested me via other people's projects. Together with Martin Steinmann at the journal *Faces*, we were able to really develop that aspect. Through other projects, other buildings, we managed to deal with topics that seemed to us fundamental, such as density, transparency, the interior. Looking back, those years helped me find myself through discussing and critiquing other people's work. I wrote a lot, and it was a great experience, working together as a team. Then I gave up *Faces* to concentrate on my first buildings, to discuss less and do more: the secondary schools at Grand-Saconnex and Pully, the Villa Gringet and, later, the Fleuret Library and the psychiatric hospital at Yverdon. These buildings developed a truly personal line of thought, and the locus of research shifted to what we were doing in our practice, Patrick Devanthéry and I. In our firm, our primary ambition was to build, and all our energy went into that, at the same time as we remaining intellectuals capable of explicitly articulating what we wanted to do in architecture. Perhaps it was those years in the 1990s that first enabled me to really understand construction, and I mean

…a subtle differentiation is beginning to occur below in the monotone of gray; vertical lines, but a degree more luminous, appear on all sides; the eastern facades of the city grow pale with light. As mysteriously as though being created, a Metropolis appears.

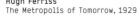

Hugh Ferriss
The Metropolis of Tomorrow, 1929

Hugh Ferriss
The Metropolis of Tomorrow
Glass, 1929

that seriously. It was these first buildings – the process of doing them – that gave me my drive to communicate as a teacher, in my classes. And the focus of my research shifted once again, towards teaching, which became an object of investigation in its turn. How do you construct the units of a course? How do you define a topic? How do you organise a class, the teaching of the subject matter? And there were pedagogical questions as well: how do you teach the architectural project?

But this again was only one more step – necessary, but not sufficient. In the meantime, ongoing reflection on my students' work and on my own practice as an architect and a teacher had become a habit. I like to raise contemporary questions whose significance I seek to assess by locating them within the history of architecture. I've always liked to follow an interesting chain of association and see where it leads, to explore telling relationships between architectural objects. I've been lucky enough to have taught a great deal of architectural history at ETH Zurich, and afterwards for a short while at the Geneva School of Landscape, Engineering and Architecture, so I'm no stranger to it as a subject. It has been a process of successive comparison drawing on the history of architecture that has allowed me to gradually identify a number of different concerns: the specificity of an urban architecture, infrastructure and urban development, mobility, neotypes of stations and hotels.

On a pu dire que la rue ne devait venir qu'après la maison, mais la logique de la ville est parfaitement l'inverse. La ville est d'abord une circulation, elle est un transport, une course, une mobilité, un branle, une vibration.

Jean-Luc Nancy
La ville au loin, 1999

Harvey Wiley Corbett
City of the Future, 1913

Eugène Hénard
La Rue Future, 1910

58 And how did you manage to translate this practice-based research into the academic context of a doctoral school?

In the traditional system, you had to accept your student topic, becoming dependent on it in a way, sometimes to the detriment of lines of research you were trying to establish for yourself. And I wanted to centre thesis topics on what seemed to me to be the crucial idea of Complex Design, and this in the context of a professional doctorate, a "doctoral school" that has since become one of the four research areas of the EPFL PhD programme in Architecture and Sciences of the City (EDAR). Furthermore, doctoral research in architecture has now acquired a scholarly or scientific status that no one disputes any more.

The idea of such a doctoral programme is that it is aimed at architects who have already had at least five years recognised professional practice. The Complex Design programme offers a training that qualifies students to embark on academic careers, to teach the architectural project and also, in terms of professional practice, to take the lead in large-scale projects.

It's a matter in each case of knowing how – when a certain level of complexity is reached, by virtue of scale, mix of use or integration into an existing built structure – we develop appropriate project tools.

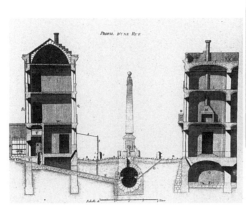

Pierre Patte
Profil d'une rue, 1769

Ludwig Karl Hilberseimer
Hochhausstadt or the Vertical City, 1924

In your own research you say you adopt an approach distinct from those traditionally associated with the human or the natural sciences, which you call "design research". But the studies you have shown me deploy an essentially quite traditional methodology, characterised by a deductive, rather than the inductive approach one might expect of "design".

The methods required to answer the questions posed by Complex Design have been the subject of passionate and fascinating discussions between my own discipline – architecture – and those of my colleagues in economics or law. We on our side most often turn to an inductive approach, which sees a hypothesis or model emerge from observations in the field, while my colleagues tend to proceed in more hypothetico-deductive fashion in developing a research hypothesis, which they then seek to validate or invalidate in the field by gathering what they consider to be the relevant data. In the context of our collaboration, my own approach, and hence my own hypotheses, have tended to converge on the deductive model championed by Mathieu Mercuriali, a former doctoral student of mine, in his book *Concevoir à grande échelle*.

To put the question a different way: these studies hardly differ in their approach from research in architectural theory or history. So is the term "design research" simply intended to mark a distance from work

Le Corbusier
Quand les cathédrales étaient blanches, 1937

Bertrand Goldberg
Marina City, Chicago, 1968

60   that seems to you outdated – because it is insufficiently close to architectural practice or the problems immediately confronting it?

In the doctoral research that I supervise, there's always an obligatory
phase of case studies. These are carefully selected in relation to the
research hypothesis. They look at objects similar in scale, programme or
context, buildings already constructed or at an advanced stage of design.
To me, it's always interesting to compare different projects at various
stages of realisation, adding a diachronic dimension to an otherwise
synchronic analytic framework.

But before even the examination of concrete cases, the problematic
of Complex Design imposes *a priori* a particular shared theoretical attitude. At LAMU, we see certain ideas, certain principles, return over and
over again, finding application in one thesis after another. The conceptual triad of infrastructure/multifunctionality/development, for example.
These allow us to compare and to evaluate our case studies – their "success", first of all in terms of their ability to withstand obsolescence, or on
the contrary their risk of causing dysfunction. Why did such-and-such a
building not succeed as expected? What is the problem with that project? And if I can identify this element, what new strategy might I adopt
to deal with it in my own project? From this emerge new possibilities of
development in design or construction. It's the element of "research by

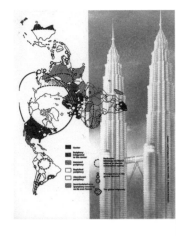

Francois Chesnais
Centers and Peripheries in the World
A Hierarchical Network, 1992

Lina Bo Bardi
SESC Pompeia, São Paulo, 1977

design" which, reflected in the project, tests and gives expression to the 61
research results.

Having said this, doctoral theses are often too long and the successive stages too time-consuming. It's essential that the research hypothesis
be formulated as soon as possible, leaving more time for project research
and the articulation of new strategies for the situation in question.

<u>Beyond their explicit topics, these investigations then represent a
critique of research as well as of the architectural project today?</u>
Yes, they are informed by both a critique of research as it is practiced
today and a critique of current processes for the implementation of architectural projects. Doctoral students each develop a theoretical proposition whose significance and originality they must defend. Their conclu-
sions derive as much from the critical analysis of the current state of
research as from the results of the research represented by their own
architectural project. It is on that basis that they develop their hypotheses, to end up with a set of propositions embedded in the project that
forms the heart of the thesis – propositions presented in the form of
plans and sections at a scale that allows quantification and comparison.
Whether it takes the form of axonometric projection, perspective view or
collage, the image becomes the specific vehicle for the communication

Peter Zumthor
Thermal Bath Vals, Sketch, c. 1993

Giuseppe Penone
Ripetere il bosco, 1970

Giuseppe Penone
Essere fiume, 1981

62 of the results of architectural research. In other disciplines, the place of these images could be taken by a text, or even a gesture. In architecture, they both articulate and make visible a process that is simultaneously artistic and scholarly.

When I talk to students about research, I always have in mind Proust's extraordinary observations in *In Search of Lost Time*. In the field of art, I'm always happy to allude to the unequalled suggestive power of Giuseppe Penone's sculpture, in works like *Ripetere il bosco* or *Essere fiume*. These are the illustrative images I invoke in my introductory lectures for the doctoral programme. They raise good questions: how do you look at a work of art, how do you describe what you see, what should you make of the title?

<u>Why the image, though?</u>
In our work, the images are suggestions, scene-settings, pre-visualisations. They are, as it were, programmatic images that communicate the innovative aspect of the proposed approach. Paradoxically, they are images that convey the idea of a project as much as its capacity to serve as a solution to a set of questions, be they urban, social, structural or formal.

<u>Isn't it difficult to present a case by suggestion and demonstration simultaneously?</u>

Avere il tempo dell'albero, della pietra, del fiume, del suono, della luce [...] Misurare lo spazio con le mani, misurare lo spazio della mano con la crescita del legno, misurare con la mano il tempo dell'albero. Il tempo raccolto nella mano, [...] contenere con la mano le cose nel tempo...

Giuseppe Penone
La structure du temps, 1993

Within an academic community like EPFL, it's difficult for the architects to find instruments of communication adequate to convey the innovations central to the discipline. A new contribution to architecture is difficult to describe, so there must necessarily be recourse to the image before built reality can take over. My academic colleagues came to understand this when they saw the images, the construction and, finally, the actual presence of the Rolex Learning Center by Japanese architects SANAA that gave entirely new form to the life of the campus.

<u>A proposition, then, for recognising in practice a distinctive form of knowledge?</u>
The university plays a definite role in practice, and vice versa. A fascinating reciprocal interaction, both necessary and so fruitful. Without this relationship, this back-and-forth, I can't imagine my role either as a teacher or as an architect. That said, it seems to me that in Switzerland the professional looks at the academic milieu with a certain distrust. It's a distance maintained by both sides. On the one hand, you mustn't be too much the professor, and on the other, you mustn't make too much of your involvement with the professional world, with business, the construction economy. For me, though, the two realms are in an osmotic relationship. At the office, nearly all my staff have been students of mine. The team

63

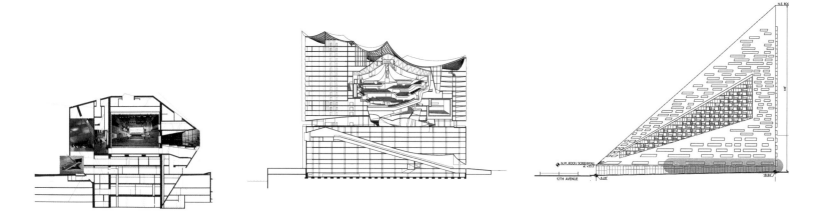

OMA / Rem Koolhaas
Casa da Musica, Porto, 2005

Herzog & de Meuron
Elbphilharmonie, Hamburg, 2016

BIG
VIA 57 West, New York, 2016

64 knows what I'm talking about. This fund of shared knowledge – the frame of reference we were talking about earlier – they're all familiar with it. They all cultivate this rigorous connection between actual, inspiring ways of doing and a solid basis of intellectual reflection. More generally, there has to be a continuity between the temporality of study and research on the one hand, and that of the professional practice of architecture on the other. For a lot of people, the dl-a – designlab-architecture – firm represents a wonderful masterclass, and I'm proud to think that many of today's good architects have passed through LAMU and/or dl-a. But it's one thing to have quality staff and another thing to raise the questions I'm interested in with colleagues, in a multidisciplinary team, and more difficult again with clients. It's extremely difficult, because sometimes you find yourself out of synch with the times. I'm thinking particularly of the master plan we did for the Praille-Acacias-Vernets (PAV) neighbourhood in Geneva, with Bruno Marchand, in 2006. A wonderful project!

In Switzerland, we very much value getting things done. You find a culture of practicality in the universities, which is, moreover, one of the strengths of the education we provide – because most of our students know how to think in terms of operating in the real world. But quite rightly, over the last few years, EPFL's school of architecture has sought to go beyond this ultimately limited and limiting approach, notably following

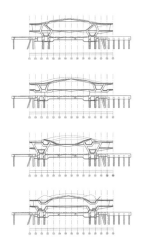

Foreign Office Architects
Yokohama International Port Terminal, 2002

Patrick Aebischer's promulgation of "the right to research" in 2002. So Lausanne students are also capable of posing questions in conceptual terms as well; they know how to think about architecture in a complex environment – complex both analytically and socially. In this respect, paradoxically, EPFL has been transformed.

I like it when schools treat architecture as a vehicle for intellectual development. Hence my fascination with American teachers, who are very often young. The university system there enables them to think in depth about the state of architecture: new materials, new systems of production, questions of interdisciplinarity, ecology, art, etc. For some time too, the relationship between the university and the big firms (Foster, SOM, BIG, KPF, etc.) has been more relaxed, and young architects are able to engage with projects on a much vaster scale. In this more open, more international context, career profiles, and notably transitions between practice and teaching, have become more flexible, and that's all to the good.

These kinds of career profile give rise to other forms of architectural practice, different from ours, but adapted to milieus that are sometimes very challenging, like New York: freezing in winter, tropical in summer, incredibly socially diverse, an urban environment marked by both obsolescence and congestion. You just can't build something that doesn't answer to such pressures! In that context, Rafael Viñoly's recent skyscraper on

It is a serious thing. […] the New York sky is blue, utterly blue. The light is white, a glorying white and the air is strong and is healthy too. There is no foolishness about that sky. It is a beautiful thing. It is pure.

Louise Bourgeois
the Puritan, 1947 (ed. 1990)

Frank Gehry
Beekman Tower, New York, 2011

66 the site of the old Drake Hotel is a powerful building. The basic structural grid, a 426-metre-high, hyperstatic concrete tube, is actually extremely well constructed, something that called for tremendous formal and technological know-how. It's beautiful, that tower! The same goes for Frank Gehry's Beekman Tower with its curtain of aluminium, its unique, glittering presence. This power of American architecture I appreciate enormously. In terms of landscaping, the monument at Ground Zero is also of exceptionally high quality: the well-judged scale, the history made present by an absence.

After the lessons of Rome, a lesson from America?
America has always fascinated me. I love New York as much as I do Rome. In the 1970s, I lived in Philadelphia, and as a teenager I was lucky enough to meet Denise Scott Brown and Robert Venturi. At the weekends, I'd go to New York. Life there was difficult and there was severe social conflict, from what I understood, and urbanism was a young discipline that sought to respond to the crisis in which cities found themselves. Since then, New York has been tested by the violence and destruction of 9/11, followed by the storm and flood of Hurricane Sandy in 2012. Over the succeeding years, the city has reinvented itself. It has implemented, in often unexpected ways, a manifesto for sustainability that is

Michel Arad
9/11 Memorial, New York, 2011

Zion Breen Richardson Associates
Paley Park, New York, 1967

gradually modifying its relationship to its geography. It has reimagined its waterfront; it has reinstated Edwin Moses' great linear parks, integrating climate-resilient works and facilities for soft mobility, cultural and social activities, housing. These projects, a little rough and ready in the detail, I really like. For who in 1972 could have imagined playing basketball in Brooklyn, on pitches open to all, against the backdrop of the south Manhattan skyline?

More than that of other firms, the work of Elizabeth Diller and Ricardo Scofidio testifies to this transformation, making an essential contribution to the architecture of public space. How do you introduce transparency between institutional buildings and the surrounding esplanade? The ICA on the Boston waterfront. How do you recast American modernist buildings of the 1950s and 60s? The Lincoln Center, the Julliard School. The creation of the Highline, too, touches on a number of the themes we've talked about, with the re-appropriation of what had been an inhospitable landscape through repurposing the ruins of a disused transport infrastructure. It involved a labour of documentation which included a wealth of stunning photographs, doing due justice to this elevated linear park with its wild vegetation sprung up where the trains used to run; a great effort of communication too, engaging social stakeholders, neighbourhood associations, cultural and artistic figures. And there are

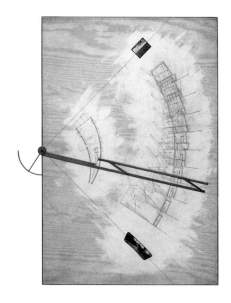

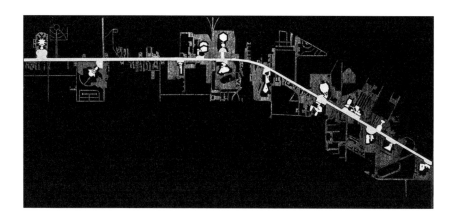

Diller Scofidio + Renfro
Slow House project, Long Island, 1991

Robert Venturi, Denise Scott Brown and Steven Izenour
Nolli's Las vegas, 1972

68   these few images in plan and section – we'll come back to that again –
suggesting the idea of a community that has taken to the idea of strolling
up in the air among the high-rise blocks. Images that offer a new idea
of shared urban space. Gentrification followed, the park-cum-walkway
being today the focus of a high degree of densification... In the metropolis, transformation is continuous.

PHASE 1: 2006-2009

PHASE 2: 2009-2011

PHASE 3: 2011-2014

Diller Scofidio + Renfro
The High Line, New York, 2014

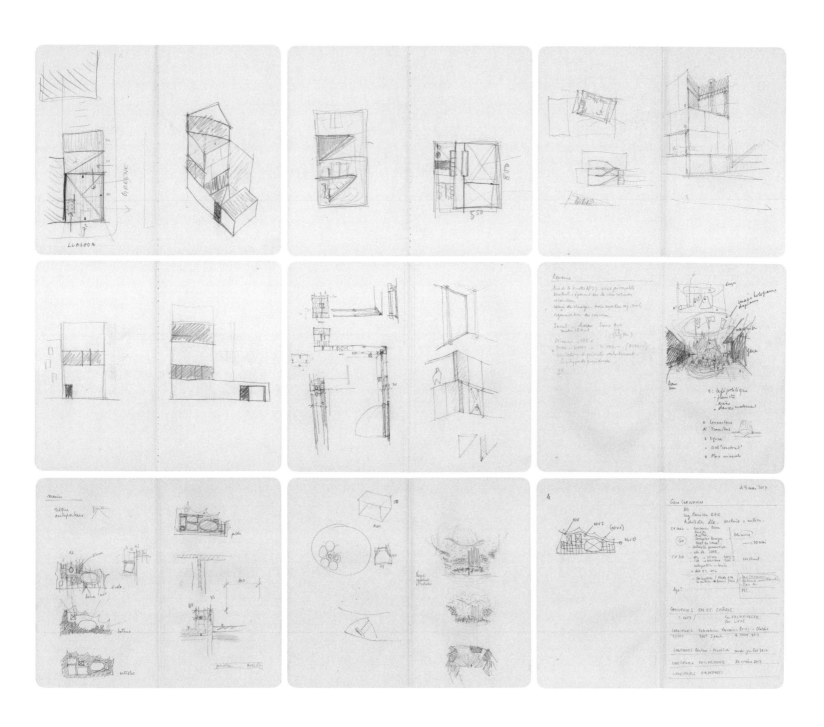

...a woman must have money and a room of her own if she is to write fiction...

Virginia Woolf
A Room of One's Own, 1929

OFFICE

<u>To return to your career trajectory, how did you become an architect?</u> You're asking me not why, but how? In fact, I became an architect gradually, softly and silently, you might say, through reading, watching and travel. Seeing things always made me want to change them, and who knows, perhaps improve them. Made me want to talk about them, too. And then I felt I wanted to make, to create from scratch. There was a period of learning architecture without yet knowing I was doing so: I made lots of drawings, I took notes, I did maths. I got to love Bologna, Rome, London and Philadelphia – the streets, the squares, the people, the cinema, the political discussions, the moments of melancholy, in Italian, in English. I really became an architect because I wanted to be independent, free to do things, to create buildings across the world. And out of enthusiasm as well! Moving on from one project to the next, tirelessly, from my first year. Falling in love with certain projects that also helped turn me into an architect: the section of the Richard Rogers and Norman Foster house in Cornwall, the glass and brick of James Stirling's library in Cambridge, the plan of Paolo Portoghesi's Casa Baldi in Calcutta, for example. But also by reading Virginia Woolf, Marguerite Duras, Heinrich Böll. I became an architect by working for Colquhoun and Miller in the London of 1977 to 1978. I became an architect because of the freedom it affords: autonomy, cigarettes, wine, friends, a world wide open before you. And then I became

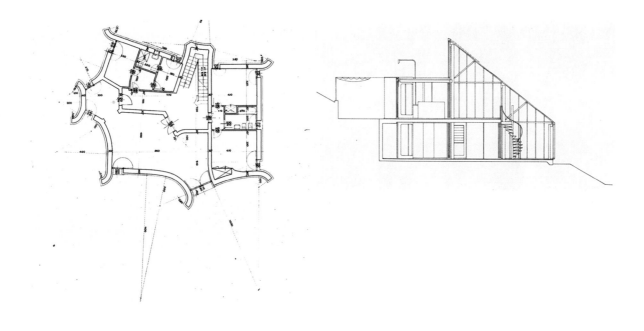

Paolo Portoghesi
Casa Baldi near Rome, Plan, 1961

Colquhoun + Miller and Su Rogers
House in Cornwall, Section, 1974

72 an architect on account of the use-value of its instruments, the pleasure you get in using them: not modelling, which I've never really liked, but the plan, the section, the isometric drawing – whose geometrical exactitude makes it possible to evaluate form, space and matter. The Mayline ruler, the Rotring pen, the pencil, the coloured chalk, tracing…

And what was your first project?
Every project feels to me like a first, in fact. I could talk about a house raised on metal pilotis, drawn in pencil, in plan and section, on the two sides of an A4 sheet. On it, my mother made a note: "Inès, 11 years old". Or another house, tall and square, set diagonally on a stone parterre whose design reproduced the plan of Piranesi's Campo Marzi. Or, finally, the reinvented Ostia of my diploma thesis, the inked landscape and architecture of whose plan extends over 1.4 square metres of tracing paper. Then there are all those imagined projects, sometimes surreptitiously sketched in colour crayon – fragments, possibilities, spaces of a life to come. A swimming pool like a beach, a school like a shelter, a hospital like a house, a neighbourhood like a factory. More abstract, a horizon line that thrums, a vertical that ripples, a cross perhaps. And I could also mention the very first projects that Patrick Devanthéry and I did together: the Fleuret Library at Dorigny, the psychiatric hospital at

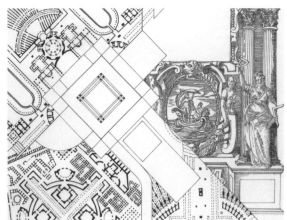
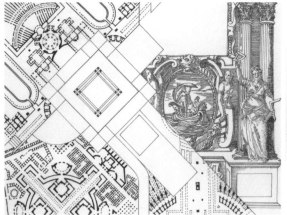

Inès Lamunière
House, L'embarras des signes
Plan, 1978

Inès Lamunière
Ostia-Fiumicino
Desert Fringes, Sketch, 1980

Yverdon, the RTS tower in Geneva, the Prieuré neighbourhood in the 73
town of Chêne-Bougeries.

The themes you mention are the same as when you talked about
teaching and research. Is there something specific to practice?
Yes. To my mind, practice requires that you situate the project as a, or
rather the, solution to a problem. In the contract between them, client
and architect find themselves confronting a complex set of demands,
expectations… hopes, sometimes. I believe in a dialogue that is gradually
established, shared thinking about how to respond to the brief arrived
at through consideration of the specific architectural themes proposed. I
can't imagine being unable to find a theme, and idea, an intention that will
move the dialogue towards a concrete solution enriched by that exchange.
Reality is an inexhaustible source of inspiration, and I love watching,
listening, identifying those moments, those places, those sometimes half-
spoken wishes. Catching what may guide us towards a solution, and then
rendering it possible and realistic. Practice is also being able to judge the
state of my knowledge.
        Writing lists. Getting things into perspective, knowing where to put my
energy and resources. A door, for example, is easy. I make it taller than it
is wide, and hinged if possible. A window is much harder. A roof is pretty

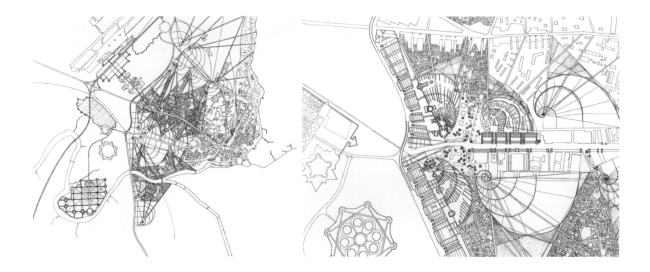

Inès Lamunière
Peripheral Geneva-West, Babylone vous y étiez…
Overall plan and Châtelaine site, 1979

74 basic: I draw it as an equilateral triangle, a pyramid of varnished mosaic tiles, beautiful, a little glittery. But a floor slab, that's more complicated. An endless tower will find its form with relative ease: after all, it's a vertical beam anchored in the earth that becomes slimmer as it rises. In plan, it will be a very narrow oval from earth to sky; it will have three hundred columns, but only four on the top floor. A 175-metre-high tower, that's more demanding. A luxury boutique is likely just as simple and quick to design: there, I can have columns like high heels, or stemmed glasses, and stucco ceilings inlaid with mirror fragments, or floors, for example, of cast aluminium. But a waiting room for a hospital radiology department is really much more difficult. The difficulty always lies in what is, in the end, the more banal, the more ordinary.

Practice, for me, is also a matter of gradually building up a lexicon of elements suitable to how an architectural firm thinks and works. Not in terms of architectural language or idiosyncrasy, but rather an inventory of approaches taken to questions posed and the solutions developed in response.

How have teaching and research influenced your practice?
The wealth of projects discussed, supported and assessed, semester after semester, has certainly influenced my practice. In some way, every PhD project becomes a project of my own: I take it in, it raises questions for

d1-a
Geneva Waterfront, La rade en scène *
Master plan and view, 2016

me, it engages me, and prompts me to try and help the student find that something that will make it belong to the present day. It's exhausting. But the attention that it calls for is transformed at times into pure delight.

My research has influenced how I think about architecture, and more especially the urban project and its impact on the space. The role of mobility, for example, in the fragmentation of space and of the social and economic fabric. Or density inducing distortions in the representation of architecture – representation in the traditional sense. I have always tried to develop projects that construct their own landscape, as I like to say. Do you perhaps remember the Villa Gringet, in Lausanne's suburbia? A house half-buried in the ground but opening onto lightwells and patios, whose windows and glass frontages only ever give onto elements of the architecture itself: an orange wall, a blue wall, a dense thuja hedge. The theme springs from the idea that the city and the space are artefacts of which the architectural object is only a fragment. Or better, that the notion of inside and outside no longer exists as such, but is remodulated in each case in light of the experience of the space. I am indoors in a public park just as I am outdoors in a concert hall.

Your research focused at first on well-known architects and renowned works of architecture: Pietro da Cortona and Santa Maria della Pace,

dl-a and al.
Swiss National Exhibition, Supersäntis *
Plan, section and spatial context, Eastern Switzerland, 2015

76 Le Corbusier and the Immeuble Clarté. In projects on the scale of Complex Design, on the other hand, the architect is only one actor among others. How then are these projects to become works of architecture?

The client-architect partnership has been responsible for interesting and fruitful project strategies, and this all the more for both sides being intensely involved. It has produced celebrated works, often recognised today as landmarks in architectural history. Detailed study of the design process, however, shows that the hand of genius has a less direct or immediate role to play than you might think. The Immeuble Clarté for example, saw Le Corbusier entangled in countless variations of both form and construction. But the end result was dazzling and utterly convincing, a crucial advance in twentieth-century architectural thinking. As for architecture on the scale of Complex Design, I think that it calls on the architect to insist on certain points that they are essentially the only one to grasp. This allows for a flexibility in implementation, a responsiveness to changing circumstances that inures the project against the inherent risks of long timescales. These kinds of projects take years, for reasons as much economic as political or legal. Getting backers and practitioners together around budgets of more than half a billion is never simple; the funding itself takes time to raise, the investment structured and timetabled, all with a view to a return. One consequence is that the dialogue between

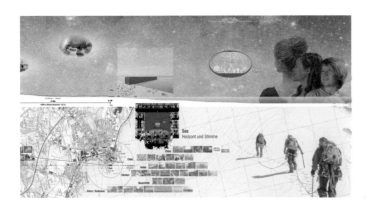

stakeholders is informed by different timescales and that some of these actors themselves may change in the course of the project. From the cases my students have analysed emerges a result that can look strange at first glance: it is often the architects who pursue their remit through the long years of these projects. What is more, it is their images (pre-images perhaps?) that seem both to resist and to profit from the prolonged time frame associated with large-scale urban planning. Euralille, Ground Zero, Andermatt in Switzerland, PAV in Geneva, the Philharmonie in Hamburg – these are urban projects where the influence of a first guiding image remains strong and distinctive, whose realisation becomes iconic.

When we have to conceive of such fragments of city – I'm thinking of such recent projects as the Berlingot development in Nantes or Le Prieuré in Geneva, our unsuccessful competition entries for the Cité de la Musique or the station-tower in Geneva or, very recently, our winning design for the Pointe Nord phase of the PAV redevelopment – our work is guided by the results of our researches on Complex Design. How do you translate the successive moments of long-drawn-out but spasmodic developments into expressive forms, into lasting atmospheres? This presents tremendous new opportunities. In grasping them, architecture has to develop new qualities that allow it to address the large-scale, understood not in terms of the repetitive production made possible by the industrialisation of construction, but rather as an occasion of variety and heterogeneity, vehicles of a specificity by virtue of which the development acquires an emblematic identity.

I'd like to offer you two examples. First is our design for the mixed-use tower by the Chêne-Bourg railway station in Geneva. Although we didn't win, the competition allowed me to address a very complex theme: the mixed-use residential tower. A residential tower doesn't share the same logic as an office tower that can achieve a relatively abstract and elegant form through the repetition of elements. When it comes to residential development on a scale as large as the tower, repetition – with the anonymity it brings – is inadequate. The other difficulty resides in the coordination of spaces ranging from the most intimate (the bedroom) to the most public (lobbies and other shared spaces). How do you organise a vertical residential neighbourhood like that in plan, section and volume? For this project, a key element in the planned urban redevelopment around this station on the new Geneva–Annemasse regional railway link, we sought to offer a more differentiated response to the requirement for densification. There were small apartments clustered around a major lobby on the ground floor, open patios set over three floors on the south facade for the intermediate floors and, finally, a large shared space on top. The roof structure deploys a set of large beams, and, visible from below, the gable ends they form

d1-a
Chêne-Bourg Tower, Tour-maison *
Plan and view from square in front of the station, Geneva, 2014

signal the presence of the community centre. The visual impact of this distinctive crown is reinforced by its golden colour that stands out against the grey Geneva sky.

Another example is our design for the Pointe Nord sector of the PAV redevelopment. For the old Firmenich industrial site on the banks of the Arve, we put forward – in collaboration with Bruno Marchand – a solution organised in section. Not in plan, but in section. It provides for a stacking of spaces, each of which corresponds to the varying conditions on the site. At river level, it retains the flood plain and preserves existing structures of cultural importance (the Parfumerie, Théâtre du Loup, etc., re-usable though obsolescent elements of the built environment), while supporting parking and space for short-term activities on pilotis; on Levels +3 and +6 is a saw-tooth roof to accommodate the activities expected in this changing neighbourhood (shops, community facilities, day nurseries, etc.), and then there are two to three floors of mixed-use live/work/studio spaces that extend partly over the saw-tooth roof. And, finally, from this agglomeration of spaces at different scales rise the residential tower blocks, themselves organised in three distinct parts: the level beneath the trees (to 24 metres), mid-level (45 metres), and above. For these towers we opted for a grid form, each floor stepped back to provide garden terraces for the residents.

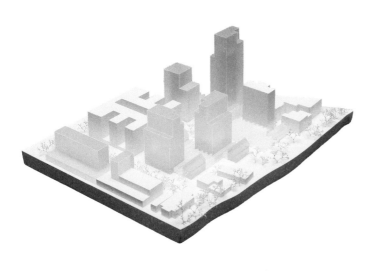

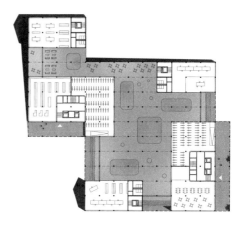

d1-a and al.
Pointe Nord Masterplan
Model, view of River Arve, section, general plan, and plan of one of the covered public spaces, Geneva, 2018—

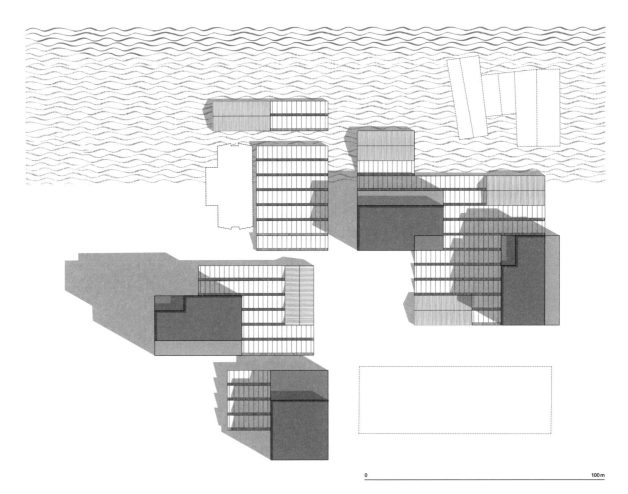

0   100 m

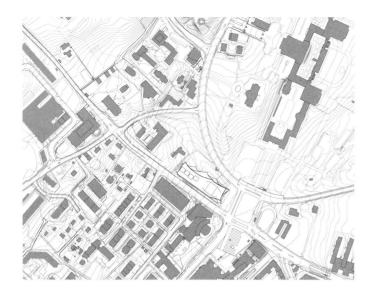

82   This approach follows on from our thinking at *Faces*, developed by and with Martin Steinmann, around the idea of "strong form". But even if I find things like Koolhaas's CCTV tower extremely interesting, for me, today, "strong form" means something perhaps less demonstrative, more suggestive. I'm probably still more interested in the more semantic dimension of form – that is, what it can denote and connote regarding its content, rather than its purely plastic qualities.

     This concern for semantics that informed your earliest projects in collaboration with Patrick Devanthéry seems to have given way in the meantime to a greater focus on the iconic, with the overhang of the RTS tower in Geneva, or, more recently, the translucent veil with which you proposed to cover the Cité de la Musique de Genève (FCMG).

These two projects involved buildings whose institutional role gives them a specific relationship to the city and the surrounding region. In both cases, this led me to look for a form that would suggest this connection while at the same time serving to accommodate a community – that of a major media organisation engaged in reinventing itself (RTS) or that of a centre for the teaching and public performance of music (FCMG). There are other similarities in terms of the internal distribution of space: in the one case, a vertical indoor street linking a series of atria/studios that open onto

d1-a
Geneva Music Hall, Good Vibrations*
Site masterplan, view from the Place des Nations, plan and section, Geneva, 2017

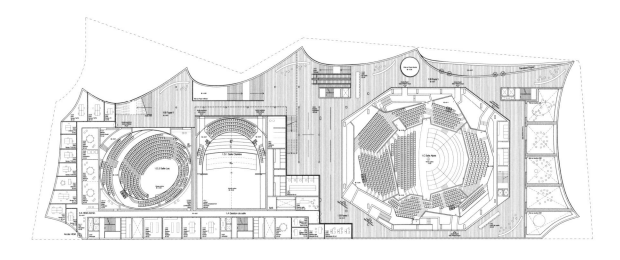

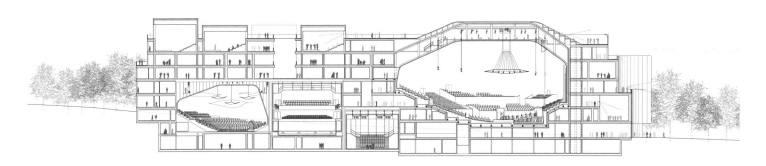

0   100 m

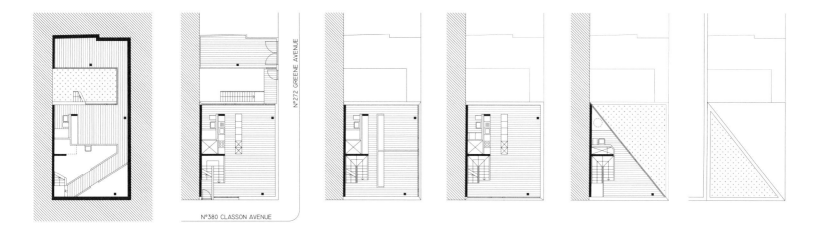

N°272 GREENE AVENUE

N°380 CLASSON AVENUE

84 the landscape of city and region; in the other, a gently sloping street with
successive landings constituting a terraced series of foyers rising through
the Parc des Nations. These are major projects serving large numbers of
users – cities within buildings. This was an idea I had already pursued
with Patrick Devanthéry, for Philip Morris's operational headquarters in
Lausanne, with its 1,800 workspaces. This was treated as a neighbourhood,
even if private, though in a less iconic style.

Since the competition for the Cité de la Musique, and, on a different
scale, my little Brooklyn project, I've been concentrating on issues of form,
where form doesn't simply derive from the object as sign, but also raises
perceptual questions through the interplay of scales, of proportions, of
form itself. The facades, or parts of them, are dynamically developed to
respond in distinctive fashion to the urban context and to shape it in turn.
Beyond a certain scale, the faceted volume, so it seems to me, wants only
to be a volume modulated by curves. If possible, a succession of concave
forms, which would extend a certain formal reflection on angularity, but
in an even more elegant, welcoming, perhaps musical fashion. The corner becomes an extended taper, evanescent, increasingly transparent as
the two sides gradually converge. I feel the Cité de la Musique is a highly
accomplished achievement, perhaps the project where the *mise en scène*,
the perceptual effects, are the most intricate. I hope to have the opportunity

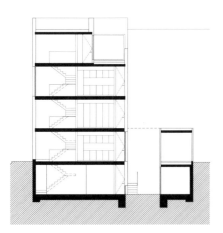

d1-a
Town House
Plans and section, view from Greene Avenue, Brooklyn, NYC 2017–

to further pursue this line of research, but a project of that sort isn't something that turns up every day.

We've already talked about my fascination with the triangle. In the design of the Brooklyn house, the volume at first sight seems simple and unified by a series of large aluminium panels. Yet at the top it is cut across at 45 degrees to the block, giving a very distinctive view from the intersection. On one side, the facade is like a tall billboard, its frontal design an exploration of the theme of door and window, so brilliantly treated by Adolf Loos in his house for Tristan Tzara. On the other, the facade on Greene Avenue suddenly drops a level as the building regains the form of a small block.

<u>And how do you find this plastic quality you're talking about in infrastructural projects that lack facades?</u>
You'll be referring to the project for a subterranean railway station that we recently won. An infrastructure project like that involves rails, platforms, escalators, the circulation of people and goods, significant environmental and safety and security considerations and countless stakeholders involved in the decision-making.

This new multi-level multimodal interchange in Geneva will see 50,000 travellers pass through each day, for whom we have to conceive an interior

landscape. I use the term "landscape" advisedly, as it seems to me more appropriate than the ideas of "internal facade" or "décor". A landscape in which movement is articulated by light, acoustics, colour, materials and structural legibility; in which dynamic and static moments alternate; in which highly artificial environments are punctuated by views of urban space; in which the monumental is harmonised with the human scale. The inclusion of activities that accompany this mobility is also a determining factor, not that we're talking about the hideous station shopping centres of the 1970s, but zones accommodating new uses: short-term workspaces, meeting rooms, gym or sports facilities, etc. Given this, I like to think that we shall be the creators of a grand interior, as powerful as church interiors, as dignified and affecting as the great central stations of the early twentieth century. Finally, it will also be a matter of articulating this subterranean world with the public space of Geneva's streets and squares, through concourses, walkways and thresholds.

And why, do you think, are such infrastructural projects in Switzerland so often won by women architects?
I don't know. Perhaps it's just pure coincidence... I thought a lot about Flora Ruchat-Roncati when I discovered that a great deal of my work over the next few years was to be concerned with transport infrastructure.

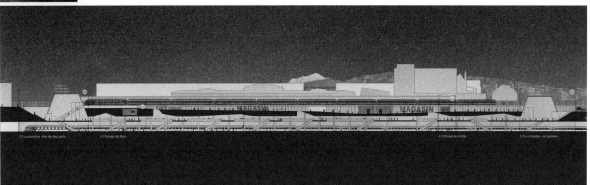

dl-a and al.
Geneva Central Station Masterplan*
Proposed master plan, vision for central square and ideal section
of subterranean railway station, Geneva, 2017

Thanks to her, the Transjurane motorway is a major achievement, a presence in the Swiss landscape. The portals, the retaining walls and the tunnels are architecturally very beautiful. You find in them all the brilliance of the woman who was my mentor and my friend. This spring, I went back to look at the public swimming pool in Bellinzona and the little school she did in Riva San Vitale: you see there all the finesse and generosity of her elaboration of geometrical forms in space. I really must go and see the big housing complex in Taranto, too, because she was never afraid of the large-scale, and neither am I!

I write from the front line, as a woman on the ramparts, but I am also a worker in the trenches and a worm near the ground. And I use my life as a quarry.

Denise Scott Brown
Having Words, 2009

PROJECTS

<u>Echoing my very first question: why have you decided to stop teaching?</u>
Because I have confidence in a rising generation of architects who will make excellent teachers, for whom we need to make room. Today's architecture, here and across the world, seems to me so remarkable and impressive in quality that I have no difficulty in handing over to them – a transition both necessary and exciting. And I'm proud to find in the built and unbuilt work of former students and employees authentic architectural responses to the urgent questions facing us today.

I'm also stopping teaching because I want to concentrate on my own professional practice at the office in Geneva, dl-a, or designlab-architecture. Over the last five years, Vincent Mas Durbec, Fiona Pià, Afonso Ponces de Serpa and myself have designed new projects, entered competitions, undergone a technological revolution, recast the way we work in teams and successfully completed major developments (Nantes, Nyon, Le Prieuré), while others are in view or already in the building. My entire week will now be available to me, for thinking, for wandering the city and, of course, for the work of designing and building.

The fact is that I'm looking forward, as ever, to embarking on a new future. I love to take a fresh look at the world around me, changing scale, exploring very different contexts. To renew sight and feeling so as to be better able to create an architecture for our time. I need the time and the

Duccio's Maestà
Siena, 2017

90 space to see things more clearly than I did before. Perhaps, too, the time has come to embark on what we might call my later work…

It might be tempting to say that you're stopping at a time when, at last, the way forward is clear and the ground has been laid for the kind of teaching you've dreamt of …
Yes, I think that these experiences of teaching and research have opened up new terrains and redrawn the boundaries, too, between theory and practice. Perhaps it's this new perspective that leads me to imagine that all the elements are in place to be able to teach architecture as a discipline in itself – an architecture that must change and develop, of course, but within an identifiable disciplinary framework. Of the three great environmental challenges – health, energy, urban development – the third and last relates directly to architecture…

…which alone makes it possible to give form to a moment and inscribe it in the long term.

Interview conducted in Geneva, Zurich and Paris, 8 February–21 June 2018

TEAM

LAMU / Laboratoire Architecture Mobilité Urbaine

ASSISTANTS

Quintus Miller
1990–1994 (EPFL, ETHZ)
Doris Wälchli
1990–1994 (EPFL, ETHZ)
Felix Kuhn
1992–1994 (ETHZ)
Thomas Lussi
1992–1994 (ETHZ)
Rebecca Lyon
1993–1999
Matthias Baumann
1994–1996
Alberto Dell'Antonio
1994–1996
Herbert Ehrenbold
1994–1996
Luca Deon
1996–1999
Sergio Cavero
1996–1999
Sylvie Pfaehler
2000–2003
Stéphanie bender
2000–2003
Fred Hatt
2001–2002
Jan Bega
2001–2003
François de Marignac
2001–2005
Jean-Paul Jaccaud
2003–2006
Antoinette Schaer
2003–2008
Michaël Darbellay
2005–2006
Roberto de Oliveira Castro
2008–2009 (GSD-Harvard)
Julien Fornet
2010–2014
Deborah Piccolo
2010–2014
Joana Leite Moura Anes
2010–2012
Raphaël Dessimoz
2010–2018
Christian Scheidegger
2011–2013
Léo Biétry
2013–2015
Xavier Apotheker
2015–2018
Antoine Vialle
2013–2015
Nicolas Jacquet
2014–2015
Amélie Poncéty
2016–2018
Fiona Pià
2016–2018

PHD STUDENTS

Stephen Philip Diskin
2005–2008
The city transforms: changing perceptions
of urban identity (case study - the path
of remembrance and comradeship in Ljubljana).
PhD thesis no.4038, 2008, EPFL, Lausanne

Stéphanie Bender
2005–2011
Le vide nouvelles stratégies urbaines.
PhD thesis no.4841, 2011, EPFL, Lausanne

Sophie Lufkin
2006–2010
Entre ville et campagne stratégies de
densification qualitative ciblée des friches
ferroviaires régionales.
PhD thesis no.4716, 2010, EPFL, Lausanne

Mathieu Mercuriali
2011–2015
Concevoir à grande échelle modèles
d'interfaces de mobilité et stratégies
de transformations urbaines.
PhD thesis no.6697, 2015, EPFL, Lausanne

Marlène Leroux
2011–2015
Urbaniser la campagne la Chine, entre
croissance massive et réalité du territoire.
PhD thesis no.7446, 2017, EPFL, Lausanne

Fiona Pià
2011–2016
Urbaniser les Alpes suisses
stratégies de densification des villes
en altitude.
PhD thesis no.7167, 2016, EPFL, Lausanne

Nicolas Jacquet
2012–2016
Londres, capitale du post-modernisme?
Transformations des modèles et des pratiques
de l'architecture dans la culture britannique
à la fin du XXᵉ siècle.
PhD thesis no.6964, 2016, EPFL, Lausanne

Fernando De Oliveira Simas
2014–2018
Télécabines urbaines: la pertinence
du transport à câble aérien
dans les villes suisses.
PhD thesis no.8744, 2018, EPFL, Lausanne

GUEST PROFESSORS

Mirko Zardini
1999–2000
Jean-Paul Jaccaud
2006–2010

RESEARCH PROGRAMMES

Complex Design
2011–2016
Fonds national suisse, FNS
Programmes doctoraux, ProDoc
Principal Applicant:
Inès Lamunière, EPFL
Co-applicants:
Olivier Crevoisier, UNINE
Jacques Dubey, UNIFR
Harry Gugger, EPFL
Bruno Marchand, EPFL
Isabelle Romy, UNIFR
Jean Baptiste Zufferey, UNIFR

Densification des friches ferroviaires
urbaines en Suisse
2005–2009
Fonds national suisse, FNS
Programme national de recherche 54
Principal Applicant:
Inès Lamunière
Co-applicants:
Vincent Kaufmann, EPFL
Jean Paul Jaccaud, EPFL

dl-a, designlab-architecture

BIBLIOGRAPHY

Inès Lamunière, and al.
.Le Corbusier à Genève
Lausanne: Payot, 1987

Inès Lamunière, and al.
Das Wettbewerbsprojekt für
den Völkerbundspalast in Genf, 1927
Zurich: GTA-ETH, 1987

Inès Lamunière, and al.
Bellerive-Plage, projets et chantiers
Lausanne: Payot 1997

Inès Lamunière, and al.
Le Corbusier: la construction
de l'immeuble Clarté à Genève.
Cataloghi dell'Accademia di Architettura
Mendrisio / Milano: Gustave Gili, 1999

Inès Lamunière
Fo(u)r cities
Lausanne: PPUR, 2003

Inès Lamunière
Habiter la menace
Lausanne: PPUR, 2006

Inès Lamunière
Green and Grey, Urban and Natural
Cambridge and Lausanne: GSD Harvard
and EPFL, 2009

Inès Lamunière
Objets risqués - Le pari
des infrastructures intégratives
Lausanne: PPUR, 2015

ASSOCIATES

Inès Lamunière
Vincent Mas Durbec
Afonso Alves Pimenta Ponces de Serpa

EXTERNAL URBANISM EXPERT

Bruno Marchand

COLLABORATORS

Rémi Benoit-Janin
Antoine Doms
Virginie Lemarié
Samuel Marie-Marthe
Barbara Michaud
Alexandre Midou
Anna Papaioannou
Iakovos Papaioannou
Jacques Edouard Perez
David Richner
Marin Thaller
Ludovic Tiollier

CURRENT PROJECTS

GAR - Underground extension
of Cornavin railway station, Geneva
Transformation and extension
of interior public spaces
and creation of two new main platforms.
Project / Realisation

PPN - Pointe Nord Master Plan, Geneva
Creation of 300 dwellings, 2,000 workplaces
and activity spaces.
Guidelines / Local Neighbourhood Plan
and Feasibility Studies

COE - Ecumenical Churches Centre, Geneva
Restoration of the main building
and construction of a new building
Project / Realisation

GRE - BASE 1, Corner town house
in Brooklyn, NYC
Construction of a small apartment building
Project / Realisation

www.dl-a.ch

BIBLIOGRAPHY

Joseph Abram, Devanthéry & Lamunière
Fo(u)r Example(s)
Basel: Birkhäuser Verlag, 1996

Joseph Abram, Devanthéry & Lamunière
Pathfinders
Basel: Birkhäuser Verlag, 2005
Gollion: Infolio, 2005

Emmanuel Caille and al., Devanthéry & Lamunière
InDetails
Paris: Archibooks Sautereau Ed, 2010

Anne Kockelkorn and Laurent Stalder
Devanthéry I Lamunière
images d'architecture: deux entretiens
Gollion: Infolio 2011

93

DOCUMENTARY SOURCES AND CREDITS

The sources and the copyright holders of the images reproduced in this book are summarised below. The order of the images used are indicated by the numbers of the page or pages on which they are reproduced in this current publication, running in sequence from left to right and from top to bottom on the page concerned.

Every reasonable effort has been undertaken to establish and credit the image copyright holders. At the time of going to print, answers to some of our inquiries were unfortunately still outstanding. In case of errors or omissions, please inform the publisher and these will be corrected or included in subsequent printings of this book. The authors and publisher similarly thank all those who generously gave their permission for the images to be reproduced, and all others for their understanding.

WORLDS

10 © Inès Lamunière, 2017

11 Roland Barthes, *L'Empire des signes, Les sentiers de la création* (Genève: Albert Skira, 1970), p. 7

12 Joseph Rykwert, *The Idea of a Town: The Anthropology of Urban Form in Rome, Italy and the Ancient World* (London: Faber & Faber, 1976)

Kenneth Frampton, *Modern Architecture: A Critical History* [The World of Art Library] (London: Thames & Hudson, 1980)

Paolo Portoghesi, *Le inibizioni dell'architettura moderna*, vol. 12 of *Saggi tascabili Laterza* (Roma: Laterza, 1974)

13 Jean Baudrillard and Jean Nouvel, *Les objets singuliers: Architecture et philosophie* [Petite bibliothèque des idées] (Paris: Calmann-Lévy, 2000)

Philip Ursprung, Pierre de Meuron, Jacques Herzog, Herzog & de Meuron and the Centre Canadien d'Architecture / Canadian Centre for Architecture, *Herzog & De Meuron: Histoire naturelle* (Baden: Lars Müller Publishers, 2002) pp. 234–5

Sanford Kwinter, *Rem Koolhaas: Conversations with Students*, from the series *Architecture at Rice* #30 (New York: Princeton Architectural Press, 1996) pp. 62–3

© Inès Lamunière, 2008

14 *Open End* exhibition at the Cimetière des Rois, Genève, 16 September to 30 novembre 2016. Photograph: Inès Lamunière, 2016

Paul Auster, *Gotham Handbook: Personal instructions for Sophie Calle on how to improve life in New York City (because she asked)*, in Sophie Calle, *Double Game & Gotham Handbook* (London: Violette Editions, 1999), p. 15

15 © Inès Lamunière, 2015

© Inès Lamunière, 2016

STUDIO

16 © Inès Lamunière, 2011

17 Peter Zumthor, *Atmosphären – architektonische Umgebungen: die Dinge um mich herum* (Basel: Birkhäuser, 2006) p. 18

18 Gilles A. Tiberghien, *Land Art* (Paris: Carré, 1993), p. 211

El Croquis no. 65–66: *Jean Nouvel, 1987–1994* (Madrid: El Croquis Editorial, 1994), p. 16

19 Peter Zumthor, *Kunsthaus Bregenz* (Ostfildern: Verlag Gerd Hatje, 1999), p. 87

Deyan Sudjic, *New Architecture: Foster, Rogers, Stirling* (London: Thames and Hudson, 1986), pp. 40–1

20 Drawing by Inès Lamunière and Patrick Devanthéry. Isabelle Charollais, André Ducret, Inès Lamunière and al., *Le Corbusier à Genève* (Lausanne: Payot, 1987), p. 23

Isabelle Charollais, André Ducret, Inès Lamunière and al., *Le Corbusier à Genève* (Lausanne: Payot, 1987), p. 16

Robert Venturi, *Complexity and Contradiction in Architecture* [The Museum of Modern Art Papers on Architecture] (New York: Museum of Modern Art, 1966), pp. 32–3

21 Karl Noehles, *La Chiesa dei SS: Luca e Martina nell'opera di Pietro da Cortona* (Roma: Ugo Bozzi Editore, 1970), p. 33

Bibliothèque vaticane, *Codice Chigi*, p VII 9 74/2

Bibliothèque vaticane, *Codice Chigi*, p VII 9 74/2

Drawing by Inès Lamunière and Patrick Devanthéry, 1983, in: Inès Lamunière and Patrick Devanthéry, *D'une géométrie baroque: licence ou règle?* (Lausanne: DA Information 66, EPFL) 1984, p. 15

22 Gail Levin, Edward Hopper and the Whitney Museum of American Art, *Edward Hopper: A Catalogue Raisonné*, Vol. III: *Oils* (New York: Norton etc., 1995), p. 165

Georgia O'Keeffe and Barbara Buhler Lynes, *Georgia O'Keeffe: Catalogue Raisonné* (New Haven: Yale University Press, 1999)

23 Cristina Bechtler and Jenny Holzer, *Jenny Holzer – Xenon*. (Küsnacht: Ink Tree Editions, 2001), p. 11

Julia Heynen, *Candida Höfer, Martin Kippenberger, Venedig 2003* (Köln: Verlag der Buchhandlung, Walter König, 2003), p. 52

24 Stanley Kubrick, 2001: *A Space Odyssey*, USA / Great Britain, 1968

Le proporzioni del corpo umano secondo Vitruvio. Held by the Gallerie dell'Accademia de Venise, Venice

Jean-Jacques Lévêque, *Piranèse* (Paris: Ed. Siloé, 1980), p. 32

Roman Signer, Bundesamt für Kultur (Schweiz) / Office fédéral de la culture (Suisse) and the Biennale di Venezia, *Roman Signer: XLVIII, Biennale di Venezia 1999, Svizzera.* (Zurich: Verlag Unikate, 1999), p. 45

25 Renata Catambas and Samuel Leuenberger, *14 Rooms.* (Ostfildern: Hatje Cantz, 2014)

Coauthor: Theo Botschuijver and Sean Wellesley-Miller, Production: Eventstructure Research Group, Amsterdam, 1969

Sigfried Giedion, *Space, Time and Architecture: The Growth of a New Tradition* (Cambridge: Harvard University Press, 1949 [1941]), p. 641

26 Marco Ferreri, *Ciao Maschio*, Italy, 1978

Stanley Kubrick, 2001: *A Space Odyssey*, USA / Great Britain, 1968

Supertsudio, *Vita, Educazione, Ceremonia, Amore, Morte: cinque storie del Superstudio* [catalogue of the exhibition *Superstudio*] (Neue Galerie am Landesmuseum Joanneum, Graz, 1973), p. 29

27 © Leo Fabrizio

© Joel Sternfeld

© Chris Blaser

28 Drawing by Herzog & de Meuron, Bâle, 2003

Drawing by Le Corbusier, 1945 in: Le Corbusier, *Une petite maison 1923*. (Zurich: Editions d'Architecture, 1991 [1954]), pp. 72–3

Fonds d'art contemporain de la Ville de Genève, *Neon parallax Genève (2006-2012): un projet des Fonds d'art contemporain de la ville et du canton de Genève* (Gollion: Infolio, 2012)

29 © Leo Fabrizio

© Inès Lamunière, 2010

© Inès Lamunière, 2013

30 Willy Boesiger, Le Corbusier and Pierre Jeanneret, *Le Corbusier et Pierre Jeanneret: 1929–1934, vol. 2*, in the series *Œuvre complète / Le Corbusier* (Zurich: Les Editions Girsberger, 1952 [1935]) p. 140

From Sophie Fiennes' movie, *Over Your Cities Grass will Grow*, France, 2010

31 Marcel Proust, *A la recherche du temps perdu*, vol. 7: *Le Temps retrouvé* (Paris: Gallimard 1927), p. 8

Jean-Louis Cohen and Tim Benton, *Le Corbusier, le grand* (Paris: Phaidon Press Ltd, 2008), p. 271

WORDS

32 © Inès Lamunière, 2013

33 Marguerite Yourcenar, *Mémoires d'Hadrien* (Paris: Gallimard, 1974 [1951]) p. 143

34 Picasso exhibition *Uno sguardo differente*, Museo d'arte della Svizzera Italiana [MASI], Lugano. Photograph: Inès Lamunière, 2018

Marie-Laure Bernadac and Jonas Storsve, *Louise Bourgeois* [Catalogue of the exhibition at the Centre Pompidou, 5 March to 2 June 2008] (Paris: Centre Pompidou, 2008), p. 145

Marie-Laure Bernadac and Jonas Storsve, *Louise Bourgeois* [Catalogue of the exhibition at the Centre Pompidou, 5 March to 2 June 2008] (Paris: Centre Pompidou, 2008), p. 170

35 Sigfried Giedion, *Space, Time and Architecture: The Growth of a New Tradition* (Cambridge: Harvard University Press, 1949 [1941]), p. 641

Lee Friedlander and Loïc Malle, *Lee Friedlander: [photographies]* (Paris: Centre National de la Photographie, 1987, no. 10)

36 Jean-Jacques Lévêque, *Piranèse* (Paris: Ed. Siloé, 1980), p. 151

Robert Venturi, Denise Scott Brown and Steven Izenour, *Learning from Las Vegas* (Cambridge, Mass: MIT Press, 1972), p. 15

OMA / Rem Koolhaas and Bruce Mau, *S,M,L,XL* (New York: Monacelli Press, 1995), p. 958

37 Exhibition *Arte y Cine: 120 años de intercambios*, CaixaForum, Madrid, 26 April to 20 August 2017

Hochparterre: Zeitschrift für Architektur und design, no. 9. (Zurich: Hochparterre, 2004), p. 28

Faces: journal d'architectures, no. 51 (Genève: Institut d'architecture de l'Université de Genève, 2002), p. 28

38 From the website www.hdwalle.com

Kerry Brougher, *Jeff Wall* (Los Angeles: The Museum of Contemporary Art [MOCA], Zurich: Scalo Verlag, 1997), pp. 84–5

Ursula Meier, *Home*, France, Belgium, Switzerland, 2008

Bundesamt für Kultur and Biennale di Venezia, *Wanderung. Camminata. Randonnée pédestre. Walking-tour* [catalogue of the exhibition at the Swiss pavilion, Venice Biennale 1993] (Baden: Lars Müller, 1993)

39 Antonio Sergio Bessa and Jessamyn Fiore, *Gordon Matta-Clark:*

Anarchitecte [Catalogue of the exhibition at Jeu de Paume, 5 June to 23 September 2018] (Paris: Editions du Jeu de Paume, 2018)

© Inès Lamunière, 1999

Roman Signer, Bundesamt für Kultur (Schweiz) / Office fédéral de la culture (Suisse) and Biennale di Venezia, *Roman Signer: XLVIII, Biennale di Venezia 1999, Svizzera* (Zürich: Verlag Unikate, 1999), p. 44

40   © Kurt Salzmann

© Inès Lamunière

Faces: journal d'architectures, no. 54 (Genève: Institut d'architecture de l'Université de Genève, 2002), p. 6

41   Le Corbusier and Stanislaus von Moos, *Album La Roche* [facsimile] (München/Schopfheim: Bangert, 1996), p. 57

EPFL: Building the Future of Learning [catalogue of the exhibition of competition projects for the Learning Center] (Lausanne: EPFL, 2004), p. 52

42   Canadian Centre for Architecture / Centre canadien d'architecture and the Whitney Museum of American Art, *Mies van der Rohe in America* (Ostfildern-Ruit: Hatje Cantz, 2001), p. 169

© Ketil Jacobsen

43   Hans Richter and Werner Gräff, front cover of *G – Material zur elementaren Gestaltung*, no. 3 (Berlin, 1924)

Terence Riley, Barry Bergdoll, Vittorio Magnago Lampugnani and The Museum of Modern Art, *Mies in Berlin* (New York: The Museum of Modern Art, 2001), p. 189

Terence Riley, Barry Bergdoll, Vittorio Magnago Lampugnani and The Museum of Modern Art, *Mies in Berlin* (New York: The Museum of Modern Art, 2001), p. 182

44   Terence Riley, Barry Bergdoll, Vittorio Magnago Lampugnani and The Museum of Modern Art, *Mies in Berlin* (New York: The Museum of Modern Art, 2001), p. 189

Terence Riley, Barry Bergdoll, Vittorio Magnago Lampugnani and The Museum of Modern Art, *Mies in Berlin* (New York: The Museum of Modern Art, 2001), p. 327

Le Corbusier, *Précisions sur un état présent de l'architecture et de l'urbanisme*, [collection de L'Esprit nouveau] (Paris: Les Editions G. Crès et Cie, 1930)

45   Robert Venturi, Denise Scott Brown and Steven Izenour, *Learning from Las Vegas* (Cambridge, Mass: MIT Press, 1972)

Robert Venturi, Denise Scott Brown and Steven Izenour, *Learning from Las Vegas* (Cambridge, Mass: MIT Press, 1972), p. 52

46   *El croquis*, no. 53: *OMA / Rem Koolhaas, 1987–1992*. (Madrid: El Croquis Editorial, 1992)

El croquis, no. 53: *OMA / Rem Koolhaas, 1987–1992*. (Madrid: El Croquis Editorial, 1994), p. 81

47   Haruki Murakami, *After Dark*, trans. Jay Rubin (New York: Alfred Knopf, 2007 [2004]), pp. 3–4

48   Jean-Jacques Lévêque, *Piranèse* (Paris: Ed. Siloé, 1980), p. 100

49   Charles Bally, and Albert Sechehaye and Ferdinand de Saussure, *Cours de linguistique générale* (Paris: Payot 1971 [1916]), p. 171

Jean-Jacques Lévêque, *Piranèse* (Paris: Ed. Siloé, 1980), p. 91

50   Martin Steinmann and Thomas Boga, *Tendenzen. Neuere Architektur im Tessin* (Basel: Birkhäuser Verlag, 2010), p. 35

Steven Kilian, Ed Rawlings and Jim Walrod, *Paul Rudolph: Lower Manhattan Expressway* (New York: Drawing Center, 2010), p. 31

51   Paolo Portoghesi, *Le inibizioni dell'architettura moderna*, vol. 12 of *Saggi tascabili Laterza* (Roma: Laterza, 1974), p. 135

Michel Butor, *Essais sur le roman*. (Paris: Gallimard, 1964), p. 57

52   Hugh Ferriss, *The Metropolis of Tomorrow* (New York: Ives Washburn, 1929), p. 73

Hans Kollhoff, Réalisations et Projets, 1979–1989 [catalogue of the exhibition, May to June 1989] (Paris: Institut français d'architecture, Galerie d'actualité and Berlin: Aedes, Galerie für Architektur, 1989), p. 47

53   Paul Virilio, *Bunker archéologie* (Paris: Les éditions du demi-cercle, 1991), p. 173

Photography: Skoeni, 2002

Hans Kollhoff: Réalisations et Projets, 1979–1989 [catalogue of the exhibition, May to June 1989] (Paris: Institut français d'architecture, Galerie d'actualité and Berlin: Aedes, Galerie für Architektur, 1989), p. 54

LABORATORY

54   © Inès Lamunière, 2015

55   Jean Baudrillard and Jean Nouvel, *Les objets singuliers: Architecture et philosophie* [Petite bibliothèque des idées] (Paris: Calmann-Lévy, 2000), p. 112

56   © Inès Lamunière, 2015

Alain Guiheux and Thierry Grillet, *Louis I. Kahn: le monde de l'architecte* [Collection Monographie] (Paris: Centre Georges Pompidou, 1992), p. 99

57   Hugh Ferriss, *The Metropolis of Tomorrow* (New York: Ives Washburn, 1929), p. 15

Hugh Ferriss, *The Metropolis of Tomorrow* (New York: Ives Washburn, 1929), p. 101

58   Jean-Luc Nancy, *La ville au loin* (Paris: Mille et une nuits, 1999), p. 42

Harvey Wiley Corbett, "City of the Future: An Innovative Solution to the Traffic Problem", *Scientific American*, no. 4. (New York: Springer Nature, 26 July 1913)

Eugène Hénard, "Les Villes de l'Avenir", in *Transactions of the Town Planning Conference* (London: Royal Institut of British Architects [R.I.B.A], 1911), p. 346

59   Pierre Patte, *Mémoire sur les objets les plus importants de l'architecture* (Paris: Rozet, 1769)

Ludwig Hilberseimer, *Grosstadtbauten*, vol. 1 in the series *Neue Architektur* (Hannover: Aposs-Verlag, 1925), p. 12

60   Stenographic sequence of Manhattan. Le Corbusier, *Quand les cathédrales étaient blanches: Voyage au pays des timides* (Paris: Plon, 1937), pp. 315–22

Chicago History Museum, Hedrich Blessing Archive - HB-23215-D5

61   Catherine David et al., *Politics-Poetics documenta X – the book* (Cantz Verlag. Kassel: Ostfildern-Ruit, 1997), p. 11

Isa Grinspum Ferraz, Lina Bo Bardi and the Museo de Arte de São Paulo, *Lina Bo Bardi* [catalogue of the exhibition at the Museu de Arte de São Paulo Assis Chateaubriand, 1 August to 30 September 1993]. (Milano: Charta, 1994), p. 230

62   Peter Zumthor, *Three Concepts: Thermal Bath Vals, Art Museum Bregenz, «Topography of Terror»* [catalogue of the exhibition *Three Concepts - Peter Zumthor*, Architekturgalerie Luzern, du 28 September to 2 November 1997] (Basel: Birkhäuser, 1997), p. 9

Catherine Grenier and Giuseppe Penone. *Giuseppe Penone* [catalogue of the exhibition at the Centre Pompidou, Galerie Sud, 21 April to 23 August 2004] (Paris: Centre Pompidou, 2004), p. 21

Unknown source

63   Giuseppe Penone, *La structure du temps*. (Annecy: DAO la petite école, 1993), p. 124

64   Drawing by OMA, Rotterdam, New York, etc., c. 2005

Redrawn section, LAMU, 2012

Drawing by BIG-Bjarke Ingels Group, Copenhague, New York, etc., c. 2012

65   Drawing by FOA, Londres

© Rasmus Hjortshøj - COAST Studio

66   © Inès Lamunière, 2016

Louise Bourgeois, *the puritan* (New York: Osiris, 1990), plate 1

67   © Inès Lamunière, 2016

© Inès Lamunière, 2013

68   The Museum of Modern Art, *MoMA Highlights since 1980* (New York: The Museum of Modern Art, 2007), p. 79

Robert Venturi, Denise Scott Brown and Steven Izenour, *Learning from Las Vegas* (Cambridge, Mass: MIT Press, 1972) p. 17

69   Diller Scofidio + Renfro, New York, 2014, from the website www.dsrny.com]

OFFICE

Images in the margins show projects built between 1996 and 2017: Archives dl-a and Fausto Plucchinotta, photographer, Geneva.

All illustrations pp. 77–89: Archives dl-a, Geneva.

Projects marked * are unbuilt, others not yet completed are in course of development or construction.

Further details of projects can be found on the dl-a designlab-architecture website, www.dl-a.ch

70   Inès Lamunière's Sketchbooks, 2016–2017

71   Virginia Woolf, *A Room of One's Own*, in *A Room of One's Own & Three Guineas* (London: Vintage, 2001 [1929]), p. 2

PROJECTS

88   © Inès Lamunière, 2017

89   Denise Scott Brown, *Having Words*, vol. 4, in the series *Architecture Words* (London: AA Publications, 2009), p. 157

INSIDE COVER

Constellation LAMU: Sources (Lausanne, 2018)
© Inès Lamunière and team LAMU

Constellation LAMU: Stimuli (Lausanne, 2018)
© Inès Lamunière and team LAMU

95

Concept and project management
Amélie Poncéty

Texts
Inès Lamunière and Laurent Stalder, Brigitte Shim

Editor
André Ducret

Translation from French into English
Ros Schwartz

Copy editing
Thomas Skelton-Robinson

Production
LAMU / Laboratoire Architecture Mobilité Urbaine
and dl-a, designlab-architecture SA

Layout, cover design and typesetting
Atelier Cocchi, Lausanne
Flavia Cocchi, Christine Vaudois

Photolithography
Karim Sauterel, Infolio SA, Gollion

Printing
Courvoisier-Attinger Arts graphiques SA, Bienne

Paper
Lessebo Smooth 300 g/m2
Lessebo 1.3 Rough white 150 g/m2

The authors and publishers would like to thank
the Ecole polytechnique de Lausanne for their generous support
in making the publication of this book possible.

Library of Congress Control Number
2018958403
Bibliographic information published
by the German National Library
The German National Library lists this publication
in the Deutsche Nationalbibliografie; detailed bibliographic
data are available on the Internet at http://dnb.dnb.de.

ISBN 978-3-0356-1807-5
e-ISBN (PDF) 978-3-0356-1877-8
French Print
ISBN 978-2-88474-694-6
by Infolio Publishers, Gollion, Switzerland

© 2019 Birkhäuser Verlag GmbH, Basel
P.O. Box 44, 4009 Basel, Switzerland
Part of Walter de Gruyter GmbH, Berlin/Boston

9 8 7 6 5 4 3 2 1
www.birkhauser.com